PREPARATION OF

Wills and Powers of Attorney

SECOND EDITION

First Interview to Final Report

Mary L. MacGregor

Canada Law Book Inc.
240 Edward St., Aurora, Ontario

The paper used in this publication meets the minimum requirements of American National Standards for Information Sciences—Permanence of Paper for Printed Library Materials ANSI Z39.48-1992.

Canadian Cataloguing in Publication Data

MacGregor, Mary L.
Preparation of wills and powers of attorney

2nd ed.
Includes index.
ISBN 0-88804-205-1

1. Wills - Ontario. 2. Power of attorney - Ontario. I. Title.

KE0287.M22 1996 346.71305′4 C96-931577-5
KF755.M22 1996

For John, Duncan and Caitlin

with love.

PREFACE

Almost two years have gone by since the publication of the first edition of *Preparation of Wills and Powers of Attorney: First Interview to Final Report*. They have been two years of great change for estate lawyers. And they say this isn't an exciting area of the law!

Haslam v. Haslam, which was reported in the fall of 1994 (114 D.L.R. (4th) 562, 3 E.T.R. (2d) 206 (Ont. Ct. (Gen. Div.)), caused much surprise when it became known that trustee investment in mutual funds would be regarded as an improper delegation of the trustee's authority. So our precedents changed to account for the impact of *Haslam* and several subsequent cases. The precedents in this edition have suggestions for additions to the investment clauses in wills to permit such investments.

In January, 1995, Rules 74 and 75 were added to the *Rules of Civil Procedure*, R.R.O. 1990, Reg. 194. These have rationalized much of our estates practice in many helpful ways, particularly with regard to passings of accounts. However, there were dramatic replacements to the language used to describe many of the estate functions. For example, Letters Probate became a Certificate of Appointment of Estate Trustee with a Will, and the Executor and Trustee became the Estate Trustee.

In April, 1995, the *Substitute Decisions Act, 1992*, was finally proclaimed after months of preparation, and the proposed legislation which was noted in the first edition became law. On March 29, 1996, in response to hues and cries from the public and given a change of government, this legislation was substantially amended. In consequence of all this, our practice and precedents had to change. Thus, Chapter 6 has been completely revised and new precedents added.

At the time of writing, more changes are on the way. We are waiting for the Ontario Court (General Division) to give its decision on the constitutionality of probate fees. The two federal budgets since the first edition of this book have impacted greatly on the law of trusts, and these budget proposals are becoming law. And so we continue to make change after change to our precedents and practice.

Finally, the 1996 Law Society of Upper Canada Special Lectures were exclusively devoted to estate planning and administration, an important event because the last time this occurred was in 1980. The level of scholarship at the lectures was remarkable, and the reader is referred to the papers which will be published in the near future.

All in all, the two years have meant that it is time for the second edition of *Preparation of Wills and Powers of Attorney: First Interview to Final Report*.

Many thanks to the various practitioners who discussed this book with me and offered helpful suggestions and good wishes. And special thanks to Fran Cudlipp at Canada Law Book whose ''tyrannical'' prodding kept me going when the pressures of work, a change of partnership and life's stresses seemed overwhelming.

August, 1996 Mary L. MacGregor

TABLE OF CONTENTS

INTRODUCTION

There are more than 20 statutes which affect estate planning and administration in Ontario. The following is a catalogue of most of those statutes with a brief description.

1. *Succession Law Reform Act*, R.S.O. 1990, c. S.26: This statute is the corner-stone of estate planning and administration. Part I contains the criteria for formal validity of wills, sets out certain presumptions for statutory interpretation of words and phrases and has sections for conflicts of laws and for international wills. Part II creates statutory rules for intestate succession. Part III provides for the designation of beneficiaries of pension funds and plans. Part IV creates rules for survivorship when two or more people die together. Part V provides for support of dependants.

2. *Family Law Act*, R.S.O. 1990, c. F.3: The Parts of this statute which are of importance to estate planners and administrators are Part I which provides for the division of property between "legal" spouses when the first spouse dies; Part II which creates the rules for matrimonial homes, and Part V which contains provisions for dependants' rights to sue for support from the estate.

3. *Estates Act*, R.S.O. 1990, c. E.21, and Rules 74[1] and 75[2] of the *Rules of Civil Procedure*, R.R.O. 1990, Reg. 194: This statute and the rules are the guides to probate practice and estate proceedings in Ontario.

4. *Trustee Act*, R.S.O. 1990, c. T.23: This statute provides for the

[1] Enacted O. Reg. 484/94, s. 12; amended O. Reg. 740/94, ss. 1 to 4; O. Reg. 69/95, ss. 10 to 13, 18 to 20; O. Reg. 377/95, s. 6; O. Reg. 332/96, ss. 1 to 10 (in force October 1, 1996).

[2] Enacted O. Reg. 484/94, s. 12; amended O. Reg. 740/94, ss. 5, 6.

appointment and removal of trustees and creates rules for the behaviour of trustees in the administration of estates. It sets out the rules for trustee investing (which are discussed in precedent F-2), and provides for compensation of the personal representative (discussed in precedents G-1 to G-4).

5. *Substitute Decisions Act, 1992*, S.O. 1992, c. 30: This statute provides the substantive law and practice for financial and personal care powers of attorney and for applications for guardianship of persons and property. See Chapter 6.

6. *Powers of Attorney Act*, R.S.O. 1990, c. P.20: This Act and the *Substitute Decisions Act, 1992* are discussed in Chapter 6.

7. *Insurance Act*, R.S.O. 1990, c. I.8: This statute governs life insurance policies, the contract of life insurance and the designation of beneficiaries. Under s. 220(1)[3] and (4),[4] proceeds of insurance payable to minors will be paid into court unless there is a court-appointed guardian for the proceeds.

8. *Variation of Trusts Act*, R.S.O. 1990, c. V.1: The Ontario Court (General Division) is authorized to consent, on behalf of minors and unborn beneficiaries of trusts, to schemes for varying the provisions of trusts, provided that those schemes are in the best interests of the minors.

9. *Children's Law Reform Act*, R.S.O. 1990, c. C.12: The parts of this Act of interest to the estate planner and administrator are s. 1 which defines "child" to include all natural and adopted children, including those born outside marriage, and Part III which provides for the appointment of guardians of children's property and for custody of children.

10. *Human Tissue Gift Act*, R.S.O. 1990, c. H.20: This statute governs the disposition of body tissue and organs for transplant purposes and for medical research, and it recognizes wills as an appropriate place to designate organs or the whole body for these purposes.

11. *Mental Health Act*, R.S.O. 1990, c. M.7: This Act and the *Men-*

[3] Repealed and substituted 1993, c. 10, s. 13(1).
[4] Enacted *idem*, s. 13(2).

tal Incompetency Act, R.S.O. 1990, c. M.9[5] were the statutes which governed the persons and estates of the mentally ill and of those adjudged incapable of managing their financial affairs. These have been dramatically changed as a result of the *Substitute Decisions Act, 1992*. See Chapter 6.

12. Other relevant Ontario statutes are:
    Accumulations Act, R.S.O. 1990, c. A.5
    Child and Family Services Act, R.S.O. 1990, c. C.11[6]
    Crown Administration of Estates Act, R.S.O. 1990, c. C.47
    Health Care Consent Act, 1996, S.O. 1996, c. 2, Sch. A
    Pension Benefits Act, R.S.O. 1990, c. P.8
    Perpetuities Act, R.S.O. 1990, c. P.9

13. *Income Tax Act*, R.S.C. 1985, c. 1 (5th Supp.): Good will drafting requires a thorough knowledge of the income tax treatment of an estate on death and of the ongoing taxation of trusts, factors which are set out in this statute.

[5] Repealed 1992, c. 32, s. 21.

[6] Act in force, except ss. 130, 131, 132(4), (5), 178, 179(1), (2)(a), (b), (c), (e), (f), (g), 180 to 182 and 184 to 191, to come into force on proclamation.

Did deceased ~~pa~~ contribute to C.P.P.
- death benefit
- other pensions - union
  - employer

- did deceased have any P.O.A. out there
- Any personal guarantees -
- any actions ~~by~~ pending by/against deceased
- was deceased Admin/exec. in any other estate
- " " trustee/guardian in any other
- does client have idea of what is content of estate
  - may not need to advertise for creditors
  - if they do not know - may need to Advertise
- Ask client - are you doing or are we doing
- funeral plans - payment of this bill
- probate - who pays
- T-1 terminal return - death
- T-3 - estate return

Chapter 1

PERSONAL DATA SHEET

Effective personal and estate planning is very much akin to a medical diagnosis. Adequate background information is essential. Equally as important as the client's financial picture is a whole understanding of the client's goals and strategies and of the family's dynamics. Effective advisors provide not only good, sound legal advice, but also financial and personal understanding and often a hearty dose of psychology.

The following is a personal data sheet form which is designed to elicit needed personal and financial data. It is essential that you understand *why* the questions are being asked, and to that end, a brief explanation accompanies each item.

The data sheet is a useful beginning for a number of reasons.

First, you will get a good picture of the client's personal and financial affairs. You will also likely come away with a real understanding of the client's feelings about his or her spouse, children, business associates and often Revenue Canada.

Secondly, if the client answers all the questions posed on the data sheet in a reasonable manner, you will be assured that your client has testamentary capacity because he or she knows the nature and extent of the assets and has discussed with you the persons who are to benefit and those whom he or she has chosen to bypass.

Finally, if the will is challenged after death by disappointed beneficiaries, not only will you be sure that you have done a proper job, but you will be able to demonstrate that proper job to all who ask. Thus, using a personal data sheet ensures the best result for your client and his or her family and addresses the issue of professional loss prevention which is a growing concern of the Law Society.

PERSONAL DATA SHEET

Date: ______________________

Lawyer: ______________________

PART I — FAMILY INFORMATION

1. Full name: MARGARET ELIZABETH BOYLE

While it seems like stating the obvious, it is important to obtain the proper name of the client. Clients often use a middle initial, a nickname or an anglicized version of a foreign name instead of their proper name. Correct identification ensures that the right will is probated and that the Certificate of Appointment of Estate Trustee has the same name as that on the client's other legal and financial papers.

2. Address: #25-88 LAKEPORT ROAD, St. Cath.

Asking for the address of the client should lead to a discussion of residence for tax and probate purposes, and often raises jurisdictional issues about the situs of assets.

3. Date and place of birth: DEC. 31, 1959 - St. Catharines

Don't hesitate to ask for the client's birth date. Retirement planning can be part of the service. The place of birth may also prompt a discussion of continuing ties to another jurisdiction, including residence or assets in that jurisdiction.

DATE OF death

4. Phone (home): ______________________

Phone (business): ______________________

~~S.I.N.~~

5. Occupation: LAW Clerk

Annual income:

The occupation of the client helps you get to know your client. You will be better able to assess financial status and the kinds of retirement and death benefits a company will pay.

Social Insurance Number - (like a file number - very important)

6. Residence for income tax purposes:

Domicile:

Citizenship: Canadian

You will have to know whether your client has tax ties to other jurisdictions because of his or her residence or citizenship. Many Canadian residents spend time in the United States each year for work or pleasure. This time spent may create taxation problems in the United States. Also, your Canadian resident client may still be an American citizen or have only given up American citizenship in the last several years and will be caught by United States estate tax rules. Finally, your client may not know whether he or she has retained domicile of birth, and jurisdictional issues arise for will making purposes where domicile of birth has been retained.

7. Marital status:

Be sure to determine marital status. While common law spouses have many of the rights of legal spouses, common law spouses are not entitled to an equalization under the Family Law Act, R.S.O. 1990, c. F.3, and are not entitled to a share of the estate under Part II of the Succession Law Reform Act, R.S.O. 1990, c. S.26, when their common law spouses die intestate. Make sure as well to inquire whether there are former spouses who might have an interest in the estate of your client by way of separation agreement, as a dependant, or by contract.

8. Spouse's name:______________________________

Spouse's date of birth:______________________________

Spouse's address:______________________________

Be sure to have the full name, date of birth and address of the spouse. The planning might be very different, for example, when the spouse is 75 as opposed to 25.

Surname at birth

9. Child's name:______________________________

Child's date of birth:______________________________

Child's address:______________________________

Child's name:______________________________

Child's date of birth:______________________________

Child's address:______________________________

Child's name:______________________________

Child's date of birth:______________________________

Child's address:______________________________

It is, of course, essential to gather the names and addresses of the children. Make sure you also ask whether there are children who have not been mentioned, either because there is no intention to benefit those children or because they were born outside of marriage and the client does not consider them as his or her problem. Your client should be aware that the Children's Law Reform Act, R.S.O. 1990, c. C.12, s. 1, defines any natural child as being the child of the parent for all purposes of Ontario law, including the distribution of the estate, unless the child has been adopted by another. It is also important to know where a child resides, since different jurisdictions may tax beneficiaries in a manner that we do not, and your client may want to address this difference when planning otherwise "equal" benefits for the children.

10. Others to be named

Name: ____________________

Date of birth: ____________________

Address: ____________________

Name: ____________________

Date of birth: ____________________

Address: ____________________

PART II — GENERAL

1. Do you have a will? ____________________

WHERE, Any codicil made, executor sign to release

Does your spouse have a will? ____________________

Ask your client to let you see a copy of his or her earlier will, and be very wary of a radical departure from that earlier will. The differences may be easily explained; however, the client's desire to make unusual changes may be a sign of growing incapacity or of undue influence by another.

Executors names, Addresses, S.I.N. -
Renouncing - name, address

2. Are you presently receiving benefits from an estate or trust? If so, please give particulars.

____

____

A testator may give, say, his son a life interest in his estate, and go on to say that the son may by his own will direct how that estate would be disposed of on the son's death, on the theory that the son would know best how to look after the family. In such a case, the son's will should contain that direction.

3. Have you set up a trust to benefit another person? If so, please give particulars.

____

I ask about inter vivos trusts because testators often lose sight of the fact that their estates do not include the property in a trust. I am reminded of the client who told me all about his $10,000,000 estate which consisted primarily of shares in a private company that owned an apartment building. However, in the early 1980s, the client had done some very dramatic estate planning, and the shares were held in a family trust. His actual estate was worth some $500,000 and required much different planning than the $10,000,000 version.

4. Do you and your spouse have a marriage contract? Please provide a copy.

____

____

The Ontario Family Law Act, ss. 5 and 6, has provisions which apply on death, and your clients may have done some planning to ensure that the Act will not affect their estates. Such planning may include a contract that they have certain clauses in their wills for each other and for their children. Also, the contract may have requirements for the disposition of insurance proceeds. In either case, you will need to know the restrictions under which your client is operating.

5. Are you an executor or trustee of any estate? ______________

By the Trustee Act, R.S.O. 1990, c. T.23, s. 55, if your client is the sole executor of an estate under administration, on his or her death, his or her own executors will inherit that other executorship. This may be inappropriate, as in the case of professionals such as lawyers and accountants who are acting for their clients' estates. Refer to precedents B-12 and B-13 for a clause which you can put in the will of such a client.

6. Do you have your own accountant or life insurance agent?

   Name:________________ Address:________________

   Name:________________ Address:________________

   Other professionals may be critical to the planning process. The team approach can be invaluable for your clients and will ensure a complete plan.

7. Do you own or have an interest in a business (*i.e.*, sole proprietorship, partnership or limited company)? Please provide copies of business agreements. Please give details.

   ____

   ____

   Particulars of the businesses which a client owns will generally include partnership and shareholder agreements. These agreements will usually contain clauses which deal with the death of the partner or shareholder, ensuring that the surviving partners or shareholders can purchase the deceased's equity. Make sure to read these agreements. They are often supported by life insurance arrangements between the shareholders or partners, and you might remind your client to review the adequacy of the insurance — it is usually out of date!

8. Have you been married more than once? If yes, please provide copies of decree nisi and/or decree absolute, separation agreement, etc.

   ____

   Your client may have continuing financial obligations to a former spouse or to children by reason of court orders or separation agreements. Make sure to read those agreements or orders since they may greatly affect the planning process. Consider, for example, the client who has a separation agreement which requires that he leave the whole of his estate to his first wife. If he wishes to provide for a second spouse and family, he will have to do so using other planning techniques. These might include transferring property to the second spouse and family by direct gift or sale or by settling a trust during his lifetime. In a case like this, if you fail to review the separation agreement and simply prepare a will for the benefit of the second family, the testator's wishes to provide for that family will be thwarted since the separation agreement will take priority over his will.

PART III — ASSETS

The recording of the assets of both client and spouse, the record date, cost on acquisition and current value, is essential for a complete planning process. The benefits for the client are many: you will have a clear picture of which assets fall into the estate and which pass outside the estate; you can draft the will to account for particular assets such as the family business or real estate in other jurisdictions; you may well find that as you discuss particular assets, you will be able to make some suggestions regarding such things as designating insurance and registered retirement savings and other pension plans to named beneficiaries, changing the ownership of the family home or doing more immediate planning for the cottage; finally, you can rest easier about the testamentary capacity of a client who can outline his or her assets in a clear and meaningful way.

1. Automobiles and boats

   Item:____________________ Item:____________________

   Value:____________________ Value:____________________

   In whose name:____________ In whose name:____________

2. Approximate value of household goods and contents:________

   ____

3. Real estate

Location:________________ Location:________________

Value:________________ Value:________________

Original cost:________________ Original cost:________________

In whose name:________________ In whose name:________________

4. Bank accounts

Name of bank:________________ Name of bank:________________

Address of bank:________________ Address of bank:________________

Account number:________________ Account number:________________

In whose name:________________ In whose name:________________

Average balance:________________ Average balance:________________

5. Safety deposit box

Location:________________________________

Box number:________________________________

6. Life insurance

Name of company:________________ Name of company:________________

Policy number:________________ Policy number:________________

Type of plan:________________ Type of plan:________________

Named beneficiary:________________ Named beneficiary:________________

Value to your estate:________________ Value to your estate:________________

7. RRSPs, RIFs, pensions and annuities

Name:__________ Name:__________

Contract number:__________ Contract number:__________

Named beneficiary:__________ Named beneficiary:__________

Value to your estate:__________ Value to your estate:__________

8. Investments

Please list all stocks and/or bonds and their original costs and estimated market values: __________

____

____

____

PART IV — LIABILITIES

This heading speaks for itself. Obviously the value of the debts can influence the disposition of the estate generally and with respect to gifts of particular assets.

1. Mortgages payable by you

Amount owing:__________ Amount owing:__________

Name of mortgagee:__________ Name of mortgagee:__________

2. Other debts

Amount owing:__________ Amount owing:__________

Name of creditor:__________ Name of creditor:__________

PART V — SUMMARY

Total value of assets $____________________

Less total value of liabilities $____________________

Net value of estate $____________________

PART VI — WILL INSTRUCTIONS

By now it should be apparent that "taking will instructions" is a misnomer for the process. "Taking instructions" is really a process of guiding a client through the will and fitting the client's personal needs to the appropriate expression of those needs. (The remainder of the book will help you further in this matter.)

1. Disposition of household goods, personal effects, jewellery, automobiles, etc.:

____

____

2. Disposition of residence and/or cottage:

____

3. Cash legacies:

____

____

4. Disposition of RRSPs, RIFs, annuities, pensions:

____

____

5. Disposition of residue (including trust for spouse and/or minors, payments of income from trust, payment of capital from trust, time of distribution of trust, provision should any beneficiaries predecease, etc.):

____

____

____

____

____

6. Instructions concerning executors and trustees:

____

____

____

7. Are death taxes to be paid from capital without recourse to beneficiaries?______________________________

Are there special provisions for beneficiaries in other jurisdictions?

____

8. Are executors to have broad powers for retention, sale and investment of assets and, if a trust company, investment in own securities, etc.?

____

____

9. Special clauses to be included

(a) Appointment of guardians and custodians for children:

Name(s):______________________________________

Address(es):___________________________________

(b) Fee agreement/pre-take:___________________________

(c) Exclude illegitimates:____________________________

(d) Family law clauses:_____________________________

10. Do you wish to have a general financial power of attorney?

____

Name and address of your attorney(s):_________________

____

____

11. Do you wish to have a continuing power of attorney for health care?____

Name and address of your attorney(s):_________________

____

____

12. Funeral and other special instructions: ____________________

____

____

Chapter 2

WILLS — SAMPLE WHOLE WILL

It is useful to set out the provisions of a whole will so that the will's structure is apparent; thus, the following sample is given. *It should be noted that the sample will is not intended to be a precedent.* There is no one will which can be taken off the shelf. One size does not fit all. However, there are many things in common among all wills, and so the structure of most wills is similar to that of the sample. A large number of the precedents discussed in Chapter 3 are included in the sample will, and the discussion of those precedents will follow the sample. This should make it easier for the user to choose the appropriate clauses from each section to add to any will being drafted.

THE WILL

OF

[*Name of testator*]

[*Name of lawyer/law firm*]
Barristers & Solicitors
[*Address*]

THIS IS THE WILL of me, , of the [City] of , in the [Municipality] of , and Province of Ontario, made this day of , 19 .

I. REVOCATION

I revoke all Wills and Codicils previously made by me.

II. RRSPs, RIFs AND PENSION FUNDS

If any refunds of premiums or other amounts (referred to as "plan benefits"), which are payable after the date of my death out of any registered retirement savings plan, out of any registered income fund, or out of any pension plan of which I may be a participant, are payable to my Estate Trustee, I direct my Estate Trustee to transfer such plan benefits to my [spouse], . If my [spouse] is not then living, my Estate Trustee shall transfer such plan benefits to my children who are then living, in equal shares *per capita*.

III. GUARDIANS AND CUSTODIANS

If my [spouse] predeceases me, I appoint my [sister], , and [her husband], , or the survivor of them, to be the guardians and custodians of my children during their minorities. No guardian and custodian shall be required to furnish security for acting as a guardian and custodian.

IV. INSURANCE DECLARATION

I declare that the proceeds of [Long Life Insurance Co., Policy No. 12345] and which are payable to my [spouse] shall be paid and payable to my Estate Trustee to be held in a separate trust in the same manner and on the same terms as I have provided for the residue of my estate by my Will. This declaration shall be a declaration within the meaning of the *Insurance Act*, R.S.O. 1990, c. I.8.

V. EXECUTOR AND TRUSTEE

I appoint my [spouse], , to be the Executor and Trustee of my Will. If my [spouse] does not survive me or is or becomes unwilling or unable to act as my Executor and Trustee before all the trusts set out in my Will have been fully performed, I appoint my [sister], , and the Trust Company to be the Executors and Trustees of my Will.

In my Will, I refer to the Executor and Trustee or Executors and Trustees, original or substituted or surviving, as my "Estate Trustee".

VI. TRANSFERS TO ESTATE TRUSTEE

I give all my property to my Estate Trustee upon the following trusts:

1. PERSONAL PROPERTY

1.1 I have made a memorandum dated the day of , 19 , which gives articles of personal and household use or ornament, and I have deposited it with my Will. I direct my Estate Trustee to deliver the articles of personal and household use or ornament described in the memorandum in accordance with the memorandum.

1.2 My Estate Trustee shall deliver to my [spouse], , if [he *or* she] is living on the thirtieth day following the date of my death, all remaining articles of personal and household use or ornament, and all automobiles and their accessories.

1.3 If my [spouse] is not then living, my Estate Trustee shall divide all such articles among my children then living in such manner as they may agree or failing agreement in such manner as my Estate Trustee in the exercise of an absolute discretion considers appropriate. Any articles not distributed shall fall into the residue of my estate.

1.4 If my Estate Trustee is of the opinion that a child of mine is not old enough to make use of such articles, my Estate Trustee may either dispose of such articles or any of them and add the proceeds of sale if any to the residue of my estate, or hold such articles or any of them until my child is old enough to make use of them.

1.5 I authorize my Estate Trustee to deliver any articles to my children at such times as my Estate Trustee considers appropriate, whether or not a child may be under the age of majority. The delivery of any articles to such child shall be a complete release to my Estate Trustee.

1.6 Any articles not distributed or retained shall become part of the residue of my estate.

2. DEBTS AND DEATH TAXES

My Estate Trustee shall pay out of the capital of my estate all my just debts, including any income taxes payable for the year(s) prior to my death and in the year of my death to the date of my death, funeral and testamentary expenses, and all succession duties, estate, gift, inheritance and death taxes, whether imposed pursuant to the law of this or any other jurisdiction, otherwise payable by any beneficiary under my Will or any Codicil or of any settlement made by me, by any beneficiary named by me in any insurance policy, plan or contract owned by me, or by any donee of any gift made by me.

3. Conversion of my Assets

My Estate Trustee shall call in the assets of my estate and may sell the assets at such times, for such price, in such manner and upon such terms as my Estate Trustee in the exercise of an absolute discretion considers appropriate.

I authorize my Estate Trustee to hold any asset of my estate without liability for loss or depreciation for as long as my Estate Trustee in the exercise of an absolute discretion considers appropriate, whether or not it may not be an investment in which a trustee may by law invest trust funds.

4. Residence

4.1 If my [spouse], , is not living on the thirtieth day following the date of my death, my Estate Trustee shall hold the real property I own and which I am using as my principal residence at the date of my death as a home for my [brother], , during [his] lifetime, or for such shorter period as [he] desires or as my Estate Trustee in the exercise of an absolute discretion considers appropriate.

4.2 The taxes, insurance, repairs, mortgage and any other charges or amounts necessary for the general upkeep of the property held under the terms of this paragraph shall be paid by my [brother].

4.3 Upon the death of my [brother], or if at any time when in the exercise of an absolute discretion my Estate Trustee considers it no longer appropriate to retain the property as a home for my [brother], my Estate Trustee shall sell the property, the proceeds of such sale to fall into the residue of my estate.

4.4 However, if my [brother] requests it of my Estate Trustee and my Estate Trustee in the exercise of an absolute discretion considers it appropriate prior to the distribution of the proceeds of such sale, my Estate Trustee may use some or all of the proceeds to purchase or build another property of any kind, including a single-family dwelling, a condominium unit or an interest in a co-operative apartment for the use of my [brother] as a residence, and so on from time to time.

4.5 Upon the death of my [brother] or the sale of such property (or other residential property as the case may be), such property or the proceeds of its sale shall fall into the residue of my estate.

5. Cash Legacies

My Estate Trustee shall pay the following cash legacies as soon as possible after my death:

(a) to my [sister], , the sum of $ if my [sister] survives me;

(b) to , the sum of $ if [he *or* she] survives me;

(c) to my [nephew], , the sum of $ if [he] survives me.

6. Charitable Bequest

My Estate Trustee shall pay to , or to its successor organization as the case may be, the sum of $. The receipt of the treasurer or other proper officer of this organization shall be a sufficient discharge to my Estate Trustee.

7. Residue

If my [spouse], , is living on the thirtieth day following the date of my death, my Estate Trustee shall pay and transfer the residue of my estate to my [spouse] for [his *or* her] own use absolutely.

8. Alternate Residue

If my [spouse] is not living on the thirtieth day following the date of my death, my Estate Trustee shall divide the residue of my estate into a number of equal parts so that there is one part for each child of mine living at the death of the survivor of my [spouse] and me and one part for each child of mine not then living with issue then living, and shall:

(a) (i) set aside one part for each child of mine then living and keep such part invested and, until such child attains age [21], pay to him or her or apply to his or her support and education so much of the income and capital of the part as my Estate Trustee in the exercise of an absolute discretion considers appropriate from time to time, and accumulate and add any surplus income to such part;

(ii) when such child attains age [21], pay and transfer [one-tenth] of the amount of such part then remaining to him or her;

(iii) thereafter pay the net income derived from the part to such child together with so much of the capital as my Estate Trustee in the exercise of an absolute discretion considers appropriate from time to time for his or her support and education;

(iv) when such child attains age [25], pay and transfer the balance of such part to him or her;

(b) (i) if such child of mine dies before attaining age [25], divide the part (or the amount thereof not received by such child) equally among the issue of such child who survive him or her, and if such child leaves no issue, the part shall be divided among my issue alive at the death of such child in equal shares *per stirpes*;

(ii) if, however, an interest passes to any child of mine for whom a part of my estate is being held in trust under my Will, that interest shall be added to such trust and be administered as if an original portion thereof;

(c) set aside one part for the issue of each child of mine not living on the thirtieth day following my death, but who has issue then living, and divide the part among the then living issue of such child in equal shares *per stirpes*.

9. Failure of Gifts

If as the result of the death of all of my [spouse] and issue, some or all of the benefits provided in my Will have failed, then I direct that any then residue be divided equally between my [sister], , and my [spouse's brother], . If one of them is not then living, the residue shall be paid to the survivor of them.

VII. PAYMENTS FOR MINORS

If any person becomes entitled to receive any share of my estate while under the age of majority, I direct my Estate Trustee to keep that share invested until such person attains the age of majority. In the meantime, my Estate Trustee shall pay or apply such amounts out of the income and capital as my Estate Trustee in the exercise of an absolute discretion considers advisable for the benefit of such person.

I authorize my Estate Trustee to make any payments for any person under the age of majority which my Estate Trustee is entitled to make under the terms of my Will to a parent or guardian or other person standing *in loco parentis* to such person, or to make any such payment directly to such person or to any other person for such person, all as my Estate Trustee in the exercise of an absolute discretion considers appropriate. Any evidence that my Estate Trustee has made any payment shall be a sufficient discharge to my Estate Trustee.

VIII. POWERS OF ESTATE TRUSTEE

In order to carry out the trusts of my Will, I give my Estate Trustee the following powers to be used in the exercise of an absolute discretion at any time:

1. Investments

My Estate Trustee shall make any investments for my estate that my Estate Trustee considers appropriate, including units or other interests of any mutual funds, common trust funds, unit trusts or similar investments, without being limited to those investments authorized by law for trustees. My Estate Trustee shall not be liable for any loss that may happen to my estate as a result of any investment made by my Estate Trustee in good faith. I specifically authorize my Estate Trustee to invest in any mutual funds or pooled investments, including one or more of the common trust funds administered by   Trust Corporation for the collective investment of moneys belonging to estates and trusts in its care.

2. Selling and Disposing

My Estate Trustee shall realize or dispose of the assets of my estate, subject to the trusts of my Will, in any manner and on any terms.

3. Retention of Assets

My Estate Trustee shall hold any of my assets in the form in which they may be at the time of my death for any length of time, whether or not they might not be assets in which trustees would otherwise be entitled to invest trust moneys. Those assets so retained shall be deemed to be authorized investments.

4. Distribution in Specie

My Estate Trustee shall make any division, distribution or allocation of the assets of my estate in kind and at such valuations as my Estate Trustee in the exercise of an absolute discretion considers appropriate. In determining such valuations, my Estate Trustee may consider such future expectations for such assets as my Estate Trustee in the exercise of an absolute discretion considers appropriate, including any tax liability or credit. Any decision of my Estate Trustee in this regard shall be binding on all persons concerned.

5. Employment of Agents

If my Estate Trustee considers it necessary to engage any corporation or person to carry out some or all of the directions in my Will, my Estate Trustee may employ such corporation or person and may pay compensation out of my estate, all as my Estate Trustee considers appropriate.

6. Real Property

If any real or leasehold property forms part of my estate, my Estate Trustee may lease such property for any term and subject to such conditions as my Estate Trustee considers appropriate. My Estate Trustee may accept surrenders of leases and tenancies, may pay money out of the income or capital of my estate for repairs and improvements and may generally manage the property. My Estate Trustee may give any options that my Estate Trustee may consider advisable. My Estate Trustee may renew any mortgage, may borrow money on any real estate upon any mortgage and may pay off any mortgage which may exist at my death or at any renewal.

7. Loans to Beneficiaries

My Estate Trustee may lend money or other assets of my estate to any beneficiary, or guarantee any loans for any beneficiary or for any company owned or controlled by my estate or by a beneficiary, or in which my estate or a beneficiary may have an interest, upon such terms, with or without interest, and with or without security, all as my Estate Trustee in the exercise of an absolute discretion considers appropriate.

8. Borrowing

My Estate Trustee may borrow on behalf of my estate such amounts as my Estate Trustee considers appropriate, and may mortgage or otherwise charge any of the assets of my estate.

9. Settlement of Claims

Without the consent of any person interested under my Will, my Estate Trustee may compromise, settle or waive any claim at any time due to or by my estate and may make any agreement with any person, government or corporation which shall be binding upon all persons interested in my estate.

10. Securities

My Estate Trustee may deal with any securities, shares or other interests of any corporation which is held by my estate, to the same extent as if I were alive. My Estate Trustee may take up new or further shares or other interests, may join in any reorganization, may exchange shares or other interests, and may give or accept and exercise options. My Estate Trustee may pay out of my estate any moneys which may be necessary for any of these purposes.

11. Elections

My Estate Trustee may at any time make, or choose not to make, any election or designation, or may do, or choose not to do, any other act or exercise any discretion or authority referred to in the *Income Tax Act*, R.S.C. 1985, c. 1 (5th Supp.), which my Estate Trustee considers in the best interests of my estate and my beneficiaries or any of them.

12. Transactions with Estate Trustee

In my Estate Trustee's personal capacity, my Estate Trustee may purchase assets from my estate if the purchase price and other terms are unanimously approved by my Estate Trustee and by the adult beneficiaries of my estate. My Estate Trustee shall not be required to obtain the approval of any Court for such purchase.

IX. RRSP CONTRIBUTIONS

My Estate Trustee shall make such contribution as my Estate Trustee in the exercise of an absolute discretion considers appropriate to any registered retirement savings plan of which I am the annuitant at the date of my death at any time between the date of my death and sixty days after the end of the calendar year in which I die.

X. DEFINITION OF RELATIONSHIPS

Any reference in my Will to a person in terms of a relationship to another person determined by blood or marriage shall not include a person born outside marriage or a person who comes within the description traced through another person who was born outside marriage. Any person who has been legally adopted shall be regarded as having been born in the marriage of his or her adopting parent.

XI. EXCLUSIONS FROM NET FAMILY PROPERTY

I declare that the income, including capital gains, arising from any interest passing to a beneficiary under my Will shall be excluded from such beneficiary's net family property or from the value of the beneficiary's assets on the death, divorce or separation of such beneficiary, pursuant to the *Family Law Act*, R.S.O. 1990, c. F.3.

All gifts made to a beneficiary shall be the separate property of my beneficiaries and shall not fall into any Community of Property or be subject to any other matrimonial rights of the spouses of my beneficiaries and shall not be liable for the obligations of any such spouses or Community. All such gifts shall not be subject to seizure for the payment of any debts of beneficiaries or their representatives while in the possession and control of my Estate Trustee.

XII. COMPENSATION

I authorize my Estate Trustee to take and transfer at reasonable intervals from the income and/or capital of my estate amounts on account of his or her compensation which my Estate Trustee reasonably anticipates will be requested at the end of the accounting period in progress, either upon the audit of the estate accounts or on approval by the beneficiaries of my estate. If the amount subsequently awarded on Court audit or agreed to by the beneficiaries is less than the amount so taken, the excess shall be repaid to my estate without interest.

XIII. GOVERNING LAW

My Will shall be governed by and construed in accordance with the laws of the Province of Ontario.

IN TESTIMONY WHEREOF I have to my Will, which is written upon this and preceding pages of paper, subscribed my name on the day and year first above written.

SIGNED by ,
as [his *or* her] will, in the presence of us both, present at the same time, who at [his *or* her] request, in [his *or* her] presence and in the presence of each other have subscribed our names as witnesses:

____
[*Signature of testator*]

1. ______________________)
Signature of witness)

______________________)
Print name)

______________________)
Address)

______________________)
Occupation)

2. ______________________)
Signature of witness)

______________________)
Print name)

______________________)
Address)

______________________)
Occupation)

Chapter 3

WILLS — PRECEDENTS

The use of precedents without an understanding of the law and practice can be a dangerous thing. The collection of precedents in Chapter 3 is intended as an introduction to basic will preparation for the lawyer inexperienced in drafting wills. The precedents are sufficient to prepare most wills of moderate complexity and value, especially where the spouse and children are the primary beneficiaries.

Because these precedents come with the benefit of commentary and annotations, they are unlike any others available to you. The commentaries are full of information and advice gleaned from my 20 years of practice, and sometimes have a little homespun wisdom added for good measure.

Over time, the reader can add other precedents for more complex situations or create variations of the basic clauses. The reader is referred to *O'Brien's Encyclopedia of Forms*, 11th ed., Division V, Wills and Trusts (Aurora, Canada Law Book, 1993, looseleaf), which contains a vast collection of precedents for almost every circumstance. When you are at ease with the planning and drafting of clear, concise will documents, the *O'Brien's* precedents will be invaluable to your practice.

The precedents in this chapter are arranged in a general way to follow the outline of a typical will. The reader should review the whole will in the previous chapter with a view to understanding the structure of a will and the flow of its clauses.

A. OPENING, REVOCATION, GUARDIANS/ CUSTODIANS, PENSIONS, INSURANCE

There is no real theme to this section. However, you will observe that each clause is here because of specific questions which were put to your client at the initial interview and recorded on the Personal Data Sheet.

A-1 COVER PAGE FOR WILL.

Short description: The cover page identifies the will and gives the name and address of the law firm.

THE WILL
OF
[*Name of testator*]

[*Name of lawyer/law firm*]
Barrister & Solicitor
[*Address*]

Commentary: The wills lawyers prepare are usually stored in their vaults. I include the name and address of the firm and my name on the cover page of the original will and of all copies to ensure that the will can be found at the firm by the relatives after death.

A-2 INTRODUCTION.

Short description: The introduction includes a description of the testator, including a statement of residence.

> THIS IS THE WILL of , of the [City] of , in the [Municipality] of , and Province of Ontario, made this day of , 19 .

Commentary: It is essential to have the correct name of the testator and any names by which the testator is commonly known, since his or her documents are often not registered in the full legal name. As well, immigrants often have a name in their original language which is anglicized for convenience.

Identifying the testator by "location" is descriptive only, but it is helpful as a statement of the legal residence of the testator for probate and tax purposes. See precedent J-1, "Multiple Wills".

The *Estates Act*, R.S.O. 1990, c. E.21, ss. 7, 11 and 12, directs where and how to file for the Certificate of Appointment of Estate Trustee with a Will (formerly Letters Probate).

A-3 WILL IN CONTEMPLATION OF MARRIAGE.

Short description: This is the introductory clause found in precedent A-2 to which has been added a statement that the will is made in contemplation of marriage to a named person.

THIS IS THE WILL of , of the [City] of , in the [Municipality] of , and Province of Ontario, made this day of , 19 , in contemplation of my marriage to , and intended to take effect whether or not the marriage takes place.

Commentary: With some statutory exceptions, a will is revoked when the testator marries after the date of the will, a provision of law designed to protect spouses and children of the marriage. However, if the testator adds a declaration to the will that it is made in contemplation of marriage to a named person, then the subsequent marriage does not revoke the will.

The precedent states that the will is to be effective whether or not the marriage happens. However, you might want to make the will conditional on the solemnization of the marriage.

See the *Succession Law Reform Act*, R.S.O. 1990, c. S.26, s. 16.

A-4 REVOCATION.

Short description: This is the revocation of previous testamentary documents.

REVOCATION

I revoke all Wills and Codicils previously made by me.

Commentary: The most common method of revoking a will is the making of a new will which disposes of all property. However, wills may be revoked in many other ways, including physical destruction by the testator, preparation of a codicil, revocation by subsequent marriage or revocation, with respect to spousal gifts, by subsequent divorce.

Be careful that the revocation clause does not inadvertently revoke other testamentary documents which should remain valid. See precedent J-1.

The *Succession Law Reform Act*, ss. 15, 16 and 17, addresses the various means of revocation.

A-5 RRSPs, RIFs AND PENSION PLANS.

Short description: This clause appoints a named person to be the beneficiary of registered retirement savings plans, registered income funds and other pensions.

RRSPs, RIFs AND PENSION FUNDS

I designate , if is living on the thirtieth day following the date of my death, to receive all refunds of premiums or contributions payable out of any registered retirement savings plan, registered income fund, registered pension plan, or out of any superannuation or pension fund or plan, payable after my death.

If any such refunds, payments or benefits are, despite this designation, payable to my estate, I direct my Estate Trustee to pay and transfer them to if is living on the thirtieth day following my death.

Commentary: If a spouse (legal or common law) is the designated beneficiary of a registered retirement savings plan, the money in the plan is not taxed as income in the deceased's terminal return. Instead, it is rolled over on a tax-free basis to the spouse, and the spouse may add the proceeds into his or her own plan. There is also a limited roll-over for dependent children. In every other case, the proceeds of the plan are included in the deceased's terminal return as income and taxed accordingly. This can create a large tax burden for the estate.

If the proceeds of a plan are given to one of the beneficiaries, it will not be this beneficiary who pays the tax. The tax burden is borne by the residue of the estate and will come out of the shares of the residuary beneficiaries. Consider whether this is a fair or desirable result.

"Refund of premiums" refers to the money in a plan which has not yet matured.

See the *Income Tax Act*, R.S.C. 1985, c. 1 (5th Supp.), s. 146(1), definition "refund of premiums",[1] and (8).[2]

A-6 RRSPs, RIFs AND PENSION PLANS.

Short description: This clause also appoints a named person to be the beneficiary of registered retirement savings plans, registered income funds and other pensions. It is a variation of the preceding clause, directing a gift to the children of the testator in the event that the named beneficiary is not living. As mentioned in the previous precedent, there may be a limited roll-over for dependent children.

[1] Amended 1994, c. 7, Sch. VII, s. 13(1); 1994, c. 21, s. 69(2).

[2] Repealed and substituted 1994, c. 7, Sch. VIII, s. 82(7).

RRSPs, RIFs AND PENSION FUNDS

If a refund of premiums or other amounts (referred to as "plan benefits"), which are payable after the date of my death out of any registered retirement savings plan, out of any registered income fund or out of any pension plan of which I may be a participant, is payable to my Estate Trustee, I direct my Estate Trustee to transfer such plan benefits to   . If   is not then living, my Estate Trustee shall transfer such plan benefits to my children who are then living, in equal shares *per capita*.

Commentary: None.

A-7 GUARDIANS AND CUSTODIANS.

Short description: This clause appoints named persons to have custody of the testator's children and guardianship of their property.

GUARDIANS AND CUSTODIANS

If   predeceases me, I appoint   and   or the survivor of them to be the guardians and custodians of my children during their minorities. No guardian and custodian shall be required to furnish security for acting as a guardian and custodian.

Commentary: This appointment is permitted by statute but is effective only for 90 days after death. For permanent appointment as guardian and custodian, application must be made to the court.

The appointment in the will should be made because it is very strong evidence of the testator's confidence in the chosen guardians and custodians. I often encourage the testator to write out a memorandum which says why the named people are appropriate choices and which may also contain guidance regarding the care of the children. Such a memorandum is not legally binding but is obviously very useful.

A parent is not automatically the guardian of his or her child's property.

The *Children's Law Reform Act*, R.S.O. 1990, c. C.12, s. 61, provides for the appointment of testamentary guardians and custodians.

A-8 INSURANCE DECLARATION.

Short description: This precedent directs that the proceeds of insurance which would have been payable to the spouse be held in a separate trust by the trustee of the estate.

INSURANCE DECLARATION

I declare that the proceeds of [Long Life Insurance Co., Policy No. 12345] and which are payable to my spouse shall be paid and payable to my Estate Trustee to be held in a separate trust in the same manner and on the same terms as I have provided for the residue of my estate by my Will. This declaration shall be a declaration within the meaning of the *Insurance Act*, R.S.O. 1990, c. I.8.

Commentary: The *Insurance Act*, R.S.O. 1990, c. I.8, s. 192, contains those provisions which allow an insured to designate a beneficiary by will. Note that if the insured makes a designation of beneficiary in a later document, that document prevails, notwithstanding that the will otherwise speaks from death.

Having the insurance proceeds pass outside the estate will avoid probate fees and most creditors and claimants. If the declaration is used in the will, the insurance is not part of the estate but can still be dealt with as the testator wishes, consistent with other planning, and the avoidance of probate and creditors is retained.

See the *Insurance Act*, ss. 190 to 194.

B. EXECUTORS AND TRUSTEES

One of the purposes of the Personal Data Sheet found in Chapter 1 is to ensure that you know your client. By the time the sheet is completed, you will know and understand the client's financial and personal affairs, attitudes and aspirations in far greater detail than most other advisors will discover during an entire professional relationship. This yields many advantages to you and your client, among them assistance in the choice of executors and trustees, a choice which should only be seriously considered after the completion of the data sheet.

Clients often ask about the number of and which executors they should appoint. The obvious first point is that no executor who has a perceived conflict of interest with him or herself as a beneficiary ought to be an executor, unless he or she is balanced by an impartial executor. Unless family feelings would be forever damaged by leaving out some of the children, I recommend against large numbers of executors because that can be unwieldy from a practical point of view.

If your testator wants more than one executor and trustee, you must advise him or her that all the executors and trustees must act together unless the will says that decisions may be made by a simple majority or that one executor and trustee has a veto. My preference is to avoid majority rule or vetoes where the group is made up of family members as my experience with estate administration shows that these provisions often cause division and strife rather than facilitating the decision-making process. For example, it is often the same two children who "gang up" to overrule their sibling. A veto or majority rule provision might be more appropriate where, for example, there are appointed as executors and trustees a spouse and a non-family member such as a lawyer, accountant or trust company. This, of course, is not to insinuate that the non-family member will make improper decisions. Rather, veto or majority rule would allow the family in such a situation to have some measure of control over its private affairs. In all cases, the decision to add a majority rule provision or a veto should only be made after careful consideration of the ramifications of such powerful provisions.

Should your client use a trust company? Trust companies are, in the main, competent professional organizations which can play a valuable role in the appropriate circumstances. A client who is interested in a trust company may want to know whether you have had any experience with a particular company; if you have not, you might meet with that company's account executives so that you can give informed advice.

Executors' fees are addressed in the introduction to section G and in precedents G-1 to G-4.

As we proceed now to look at the precedents for executors and trustees, note that each clause refers to the executor and trustee (original, substitute or surviving) by the generic term "Estate Trustee". This is for convenience of drafting only and also because the new Rules 74[3] and 75[4] of the *Rules of Civil Procedure*, R.R.O. 1990, Reg. 194, refer to the appointment of an "estate trustee with a will" rather than to an executor and trustee. The previous edition of this book and many practitioners still prefer the generic term "Trustee".

B-1 EXECUTOR AND TRUSTEE — NO SUBSTITUTE.

Short description: One person (or trust company) is appointed as the executor and trustee.

EXECUTOR AND TRUSTEE

I appoint to be the Executor and Trustee of my Will and I will refer to the Executor and Trustee as my "Estate Trustee".

Commentary: I usually recommend against an individual being appointed in this way. I prefer the inclusion of substitutes and refer you to precedents B-2, B-3 and B-5. It is, however, appropriate to appoint a trust company by this clause, since it is less likely that a substitute will be necessary.

The *Trustee Act*, R.S.O. 1990, c. T.23, s. 3(1), provides for the

[3] Enacted O. Reg. 484/94, s. 12; amended O. Reg. 740/94, ss. 1 to 4; O. Reg. 69/95, ss. 10 to 13, 18 to 20; O. Reg. 377/95, s. 6; O. Reg. 332/96, ss. 1-10 (in force October 1, 1996).

[4] Enacted O. Reg. 484/94, s. 12; amended O. Reg. 740/94, ss. 5, 6.

appointment of a new trustee in place of a sole trustee who dies, remains outside Ontario for more than 12 months, wants to be discharged, is unfit or refuses to act. Section 4 gives a sole trustee the right to appoint a successor by his or her will.

B-2 EXECUTOR AND TRUSTEE — ONE SUBSTITUTE.

Short description: One executor and trustee is appointed, with one named substitute.

EXECUTOR AND TRUSTEE

I appoint to be the Executor and Trustee of my Will. If does not survive me or otherwise is or becomes unwilling or unable to act as my Executor and Trustee before all the trusts set out in my Will have been fully performed, I appoint to be the Executor and Trustee of my Will.

In my Will, I refer to the Executor and Trustee, original or substituted, as my "Estate Trustee".

Commentary: This is the most typical clause where the estate is of modest value and average complexity. It also addresses the problem, mentioned in the commentary to precedent B-1, of a sole trustee being appointed with no substitute provided.

B-3 EXECUTOR AND TRUSTEE — TWO OR MORE SUBSTITUTES.

Short description: One executor and trustee is appointed, with provision for two (or more, if desired) substitutes if the first is unwilling or unable to act.

> **EXECUTOR AND TRUSTEE**
>
> I appoint to be the Executor and Trustee of my Will. If does not survive me or is or becomes unwilling or unable to act as my Executor and Trustee before all the trusts set out in my Will have been fully performed, I appoint and to be the Executors and Trustees of my Will.
>
> In my Will, I refer to the Executor and Trustee or Executors and Trustees, original or substituted or surviving, as my "Estate Trustee".

Commentary: This precedent allows for two or more substitutes. I often use this clause where a testator wishes to appoint the spouse, with all of his or her children as substitutes. Such an appointment preserves family harmony, although it may prove unmanageable as a practical matter.

B-4 EXECUTOR AND TRUSTEE — MAJORITY RULE.

Short description: This clause provides that a decision may be made by a simple majority.

EXECUTOR AND TRUSTEE

If any difference of opinion arises among my Estate Trustees in relation to the execution of the trusts of my Will, the opinion of the majority of them shall prevail [whether or not an Estate Trustee may be personally interested or concerned in the matter in dispute or question].

Commentary: This paragraph might be added to any of the appointments of more than one executor and trustee. Please refer to the introduction to this section for my comments about majority rule and vetoes.

B-5 EXECUTOR AND TRUSTEE — TWO SUCCESSIVE SUBSTITUTES.

Short description: This clause appoints one original executor and trustee, one substitute and a second substitute.

EXECUTOR AND TRUSTEE

I appoint   to be the Executor and Trustee of my Will. If   does not survive me or is or becomes unwilling or unable to act as my Executor and Trustee before all the trusts set out in my Will have been fully performed, I appoint   to be the Executor and Trustee.

If   does not survive me or is or becomes unwilling or unable to act before all the trusts are fully performed, I appoint to be the Executor and Trustee of my Will.

I will refer to the Executor and Trustee of my Will, original or substituted, as my "Estate Trustee".

Commentary: This is a useful variation of precedent B-6. It ensures an unbroken chain of executorship. I would likely use this precedent if the first and second executors and trustees are elderly or about the same age as the testator.

B-6 TWO EXECUTORS AND TRUSTEES — NO SUBSTITUTE.

Short description: Two original executors and trustees are appointed. There is no provision for a substitute.

EXECUTORS AND TRUSTEES

I appoint and to be the Executors and Trustees of my Will. I will refer to the Executor and Trustee or Executors and Trustees as my "Estate Trustees".

Commentary: If one of these named executors and trustees dies, the other is entitled to continue as the sole executor and trustee.

See the *Trustee Act*, s. 3.

B-7 TWO EXECUTORS AND TRUSTEES — ONE SUBSTITUTE.

Short description: Two executors and trustees are appointed, with provision for one substitute.

EXECUTORS AND TRUSTEES

I appoint   and   to be the Executors and Trustees of my Will. If either   or   predeceases me or dies before all the trusts set out in my Will have been completed, or is or becomes unwilling or unable to act or continue to act as an Executor and Trustee, then I appoint   to be a co-executor and a co-trustee in   's place.

I will refer to the Executors and Trustees of my Will, whether original or substituted, as my "Estate Trustees".

Commentary: The substitute executor and trustee may replace one or both of the original executors and trustees. This is a useful clause when the surviving spouse is one of the executors and trustees of trusts created for his or her benefit, since the spouse may have a conflict of interest.

B-8 MULTIPLE EXECUTORS AND TRUSTEES — ACTIVE TRUSTEE'S DUTIES.

Short description: One of the executors and trustees is directed to keep the books and records and to have custody of the assets.

shall take upon itself the accounting duties and the day-to-day procedural responsibilities of my estate and shall keep in its custody all the assets of my estate.

Commentary: This precedent is added to appointments where one of two or more co-executors and co-trustees is a professional trustee, usually a trust company.

At law, a trustee is forbidden to delegate his or her responsibility to a co-trustee unless the will permits it. This precedent, however, delegates administrative responsibility only and does not defeat the anti-delegation rule.

See *Fales v. Canada Permanent Trust Co.* (1976), 70 D.L.R. (3d) 257, [1977] 2 S.C.R. 302, where a widow, who was a co-trustee with the trust company, left the administration of the estate to her co-trustee.

B-9 REMOVAL OF EXECUTOR AND TRUSTEE SPOUSE WHO ELECTS EQUALIZATION.

Short description: Added to the appointment of the surviving spouse as an executor and trustee, this precedent ensures the removal of that spouse if he or she moves against the estate under s. 6 of the *Family Law Act*, R.S.O. 1990, c. F.3.

If at any time within six months following the date of my death, my [wife] makes an election under the *Family Law Act*, R.S.O. 1990, c. F.3, or its successor Act, to receive any entitlement to my net family property as defined in the Act, my [wife] shall immediately cease to be an Executor and Trustee of my Will.

I appoint   to be an Executor and Trustee in the place of my [wife]. My Will shall be construed and take effect as if   had been originally appointed as my Executor and Trustee.

Commentary: A spouse obviously cannot act both for and against the estate. Section 6 of the *Family Law Act* provides that on the death of one spouse, the surviving spouse may elect to take the benefits under the Act rather than the gifts under the will. The estate is *not* entitled to move against a surviving spouse. "Spouse" means a legal spouse only.

This is a complex area of the law. I refer you to two excellent reference texts: B. Hovius and T.G. Youdan, *Law of Family Property* (Toronto, Carswell, 1991), Part II, and A.H. Oosterhoff, *Wills and Succession*, 3rd ed. (Toronto, Carswell, 1991), Part V.

B-10 RESIGNATION OF EXECUTOR AND TRUSTEE.

Short description: This clause provides that trustees may resign on 30 days notice.

RESIGNATION OF EXECUTOR AND TRUSTEE

An Estate Trustee may resign on 30 days written notice to the other Estate Trustees and to the next-appointed Estate Trustees. No Estate Trustee who resigns shall be required to pass accounts, and the next-appointed Estate Trustee shall be liable only for the assets which are delivered to [him] by the Estate Trustee so resigning.

Commentary: A trustee sometimes wishes to resign, often when the will has created long-term trusts and several years have passed. The trustee might be moving away or simply be worn out by the demands of the administration or more likely of the beneficiaries. Such a trustee, but for this paragraph, would require court approval and would have to prepare accounts of his or her administration.

B-11 REMOVAL OF EXECUTOR AND TRUSTEE.

Short description: This clause provides that trustees may remove one of their number.

REMOVAL OF EXECUTOR AND TRUSTEE

If there are three or more Estate Trustees and it is the opinion of all of them other than the one to be removed that the best interests of my estate require the resignation or removal of an Estate Trustee, then the written determination by all such Estate Trustees shall be effective in terminating the appointment of such Estate Trustee.

Commentary: This is a fairly draconian measure. Please see my comments at the beginning of this section about majority rule and vetoes. This clause is similar in effect to a majority rule or veto clause, but might be appropriate in limited circumstances. Such a removal, but for this paragraph, would require court approval and accounts of the administration.

B-12 MY EXECUTOR AND TRUSTEE TO BE TRUSTEE OF OTHER ESTATES.

Short description: This precedent provides for the appointment of a successor trustee for estates of which the testator is the sole trustee.

> **TRUSTEE OF OTHER ESTATES**
>
> For those estates of which I am the sole Estate Trustee or the sole surviving Estate Trustee, except the estates of my [husband] and any person related to me by blood or marriage or adoption, I appoint my colleague, , to be the successor Executor and Trustee. If my colleague, , is not then living, or is or becomes unwilling or unable to act as the Executor and Trustee, I appoint my colleague, , to be such Executor and Trustee.

Commentary: I sometimes will act as trustee for my clients. I have inserted this clause in my will to ensure that my husband and my children are not burdened with the administration of my clients' estates. Rather, I ensure that my colleague is appointed. The colleague can be named, but it might be preferable to give the partners of the firm the right to appoint a substitute. The wording of such a clause must be crystal clear to avoid having it declared void for uncertainty. Similar provision for a substitute should be made in the client's will (see precedents B-2, B-3, B-5 and B-7.

See the *Trustee Act*, s. 55, which provides that the executor and trustee of the sole surviving trustee inherits the unfinished administration.

B-13 EXECUTOR AND TRUSTEE APPOINTS A SUCCESSOR.

Short description: This clause provides that a sole trustee or sole surviving trustee may appoint a successor trustee.

APPOINTMENT OF SUCCESSOR EXECUTOR AND TRUSTEE

For those estates of which I am the sole Estate Trustee or sole remaining Estate Trustee [except for the estates of my husband and any other person related to me by blood or marriage], I appoint [my colleague, ,] to be the successor Estate Trustee. If [my colleague, ,] is not then living, or is or becomes unwilling or unable to act as the Estate Trustee, I appoint [my colleague, ,] to be the Estate Trustee.

Commentary: If the sole trustee or sole remaining trustee dies during the term of his or her administration, the chain of administration is not broken by reason of that death. The rule is that the executor and trustee appointed by the will of the sole trustee or sole remaining trustee becomes the trustee of the first estate. If you are acting as the trustee for the estates of your clients, you may not want your spouse or other family member to be the substituted trustee for your clients' estates. This clause ensures that you can appoint a partner or other colleague for the clients' estates.

B-14 TRUSTEE CHANGE WHEN EXECUTOR'S WORK IS FINISHED.

Short description: This clause can be added to the earlier appointments if the testator wants a different trustee for the trusts created by the will.

> If my Estate Trustee has determined that [he] has completed [his] duties as the Executor and holds the balance of the estate as a trustee only, I authorize [him] to appoint to be a trustee with [him]. shall have the same powers and discretions as I have given to my Estate Trustee. A recital by my Estate Trustee that [he] has completed [his] duties as executor shall be conclusive proof of the fact.

Commentary: See *McLean (Re)* (1982), 135 D.L.R. (3d) 667, 37 O.R. (2d) 164 (H.C.J.), which holds that the person or corporation appointed as the executor and trustee is *both* executor and trustee throughout the administration of the estate.

C. BEQUESTS/DEVISES/LEGACIES, DEBTS/DEATH TAXES

There is very little common theme among the precedents which appear in this section. The individual commentaries are lengthy, and there are many annotations.

In a general way, clients often struggle with the decisions surrounding the disposition of their personal effects. It has long been my experience that it is over such disposition that the nastiest fights occur between family members, fights which can be carried on for years. It is at this point in the planning where your clients must think long and hard about their children and plan to help them rather than create conflicts and divisions.

Real property which is held for a beneficiary creates its own problems. The usual problems occur when the will is silent about the possibility of future events. Neighbourhoods change, properties deteriorate, people's lives go on, and the estate which is saddled with real estate can be a burden for the beneficiaries and the trustees. Because of this, it is my view that real estate trusts should be used sparingly.

Then there is the cottage. More real estate to worry about, only this time it comes packed with all the emotion and nostalgia of every child who has ever grown up with a cottage. I usually recommend against elaborate arrangements for sharing a cottage among children. Such arrangements are often doomed. However, if carefully planned, perhaps with the participation of the children, cottage arrangements can work well and create long-term sharing and sometimes tax relief. It is a good idea to invite the participation of a tax lawyer or accountant in drafting such arrangements.

Cash legacies are made for the usual charitable and sentimental reasons. Make sure to obtain full particulars of all the legatees to ensure that they will be found after death. I often recommend legacies for those people who have moral or legal claims against the estate as a means of avoiding legal action. This may, of course, not be effective; however, immediate cash is often preferable to a protracted wait.

C-1 TRANSFERS TO TRUSTEE.

Short description: All property of the deceased is directed to be transferred to the trustee.

> **TRANSFERS TO ESTATE TRUSTEE**
>
> I give all my property to my Estate Trustee upon the following trusts:

Variation: A more traditional clause attempts to broaden the definition of "property" to ensure that there is no issue about what assets form the estate.

> **TRANSFERS TO ESTATE TRUSTEE**
>
> I give all my property of every nature and kind wherever situate, both real and personal and including any property over which I may have a general power of appointment, to my Estate Trustee upon the following trusts:

Commentary: The trustee is unique to English common law because of title to property being divided, the trustee having legal title and the beneficiaries having beneficial title. The trustee named in the will has legal title to the assets of the deceased, but only to carry out the trusts directed by the will.

Section 9 of the *Trustee Act* vests legal title to the assets of the deceased in the trustee.

C-2 PERSONAL PROPERTY TO NAMED BENEFICIARY.

Short description: This clause gives all personal effects, household goods and vehicles to a named beneficiary who must survive for 30 days in order to inherit.

> **PERSONAL PROPERTY**
>
> If   is living on the thirtieth day following my death, my Estate Trustee shall transfer and deliver to   all articles of personal and household use or ornament, and all automobiles and accessories thereto, then owned by me.

Commentary: This is a typical clause in spousal wills. Each spouse gives the other all the personal effects, etc., since it is almost impossible to determine ownership of such articles. It is likely correct to assume that such articles are held jointly between the spouses and therefore pass outside the will in any event.

You should discuss with the testator whether there are any special articles which have monetary or sentimental value and which should therefore be made the subject of a special gift. This can be done by using precedent C-4 to make such gifts by memorandum, or by referring to such gifts in the will.

See the introduction to section D for a discussion of the 30-day survivorship period, and see the annotation to precedent C-3 for practice tips.

C-3 SPECIFIED PERSONAL PROPERTY TO NAMED BENEFICIARY.

Short description: This clause disposes of specific personal effects and household goods to a named beneficiary.

> **PERSONAL PROPERTY**
>
> My Estate Trustee shall transfer and deliver to , if survives me, [*specify articles*].

Commentary: There are four important points for this clause and indeed for all gifts of personal property:

1. The general rule is that the will "speaks from death" rather than from the date of the will. While there are exceptions, the issue at the planning stage is to discuss with the testator the possibility of a given article of personal property not existing at the date of death.

2. The precedent given here provides that the beneficiary will only take if alive at the date of death. You must discuss the possibility of the beneficiary not being alive at the death of the testator, and draft the clause to deal with that event.

3. It is your job to ensure that specific property is described properly in the will so that it can be identified after death.

4. You are reminded to avoid gifts of "contents" of a room, a locked box, a desk, etc. These kinds of gifts invite interpretation problems if the gift happens not to be in the place specified or if additional property is inadvertently in the place referred to.

See s. 22 of the *Succession Law Reform Act* (will speaks from death) and s. 23 (disposition where the beneficiary dies in the lifetime of the deceased). See also *Rutherford (Re)* (1918), 42 O.L.R. 405, 14 O.W.N. 40 (H.C.), which is often cited to support s. 22.

C-4 INCORPORATION OF MEMORANDUM OF PERSONAL PROPERTY.

Short description: A list or memorandum "incorporated" into the will disposes of specific articles to named beneficiaries.

> **PERSONAL PROPERTY**
>
> I have made a memorandum dated the day of , 19 , which gives articles of personal and household use or ornament, and I have deposited it with my Will. I direct my Estate Trustee to deliver the articles of personal and household use or ornament described in the memorandum in accordance with the memorandum.

Commentary: There are three conditions for an unattested document to be incorporated into a will: the document must exist prior to the execution of the will; the will must refer to it as an existing document, and the document must be sufficiently described to be identified.

You will want to consider whether the memorandum should be incorporated. If the memorandum is incorporated using this precedent, it cannot be changed without formal amendment to the will, either by codicil or by a new will. This can be inconvenient, and so it is useful to discuss with your client non-binding methods of having the beneficiaries deal with various articles. For example, a list in Mother's handwriting can be very persuasive, and the children will honour it because it is what their mother wished them to do. If, however, the testator has decided to incorporate a list, remind him or her to address the issue of a beneficiary predeceasing.

There are several Ontario decisions which refer to the doctrine of incorporation of unattested documents into wills. The most interesting case is *Coate Estate (Re)* (1987), 26 E.T.R. 161 (Ont. Surr. Ct.), which was a clever but finally unsuccessful attempt by counsel to argue that handwritten alterations on a will were intended to be a holograph codicil which would be incorporated into the old will.

C-5 RIGHT TO SELECT ITEMS OF PERSONAL PROPERTY.

Short description: A named beneficiary is allowed to select personal or household articles.

> **PERSONAL PROPERTY**
>
> My Estate Trustee shall allow , if survives me, to choose any articles of personal and household use or ornament belonging to me at my death. The articles which does not want shall become part of the residue of my estate.

Commentary: This precedent creates an unrestricted right in a beneficiary to select personal or household articles. Your client might want to limit the number of choices or add to the beneficiaries. If several beneficiaries have the right to choose, it is a good idea to make some rules, such as drawing straws for the first choice.

See precedents C-6, C-7 and C-8 for precedents concerning divisions among children.

C-6 PERSONAL PROPERTY — OUTRIGHT TO ONE BENEFICIARY; GIFT OVER TO CHILDREN.

Short description: Under this precedent, a named beneficiary, usually the spouse, will inherit all personal effects and household goods if living on the thirtieth day following the date of death. If the spouse is not living, the articles will be divided among the children of the testator. If the children fight, the estate trustee will settle the dispute.

PERSONAL PROPERTY

My Estate Trustee shall deliver to if is living on the thirtieth day following the date of my death, all articles of personal and household use or ornament, and all automobiles and their accessories.

If is not then living, my Estate Trustee shall divide all such articles among my children then living in such manner as they may agree, or failing agreement, in such manner as my Estate Trustee in the exercise of an absolute discretion considers appropriate. Any articles not distributed shall fall into the residue of my estate.

Commentary: As mentioned in the introduction to this section, division of the deceased's property can cause bad feelings among the children long after the event. There needs to be a mechanism for orderly distribution among the children, with the trustee able to settle disputes, or better yet, able to threaten that disputed articles will be sold. The testator may want to create rules for distribution.

C-7 PERSONAL PROPERTY — DIVISION AMONG CHILDREN.

Short description: Children of the deceased are permitted to divide personal and household effects among themselves. The trustee has power to settle disputes.

PERSONAL PROPERTY

My Estate Trustee shall divide all articles of personal and household use or ornament, and all automobiles and their accessories, among my children then living in such manner as they may agree, or failing agreement, in such manner as my Estate Trustee in the exercise of an absolute discretion considers appropriate. Any articles not distributed shall become part of the residue of my estate.

Commentary: This is basically the same distribution as in precedent C-6, only here there is no surviving spouse to be considered. Who would envy this trustee the role of settling the children's disputes? One strategy the trustee might use is the threat that disputed articles will be sold — this usually creates a fast settlement of differences.

C-8 TRUSTEE TO HOLD PERSONAL PROPERTY FOR MINOR.

Short description: The trustee is given discretion to manage and dispose of personal and household effects for minors.

If my Estate Trustee is of the opinion that a child of mine is not old enough to make use of such articles, my Estate Trustee may either dispose of such articles or any of them and add the proceeds of sale if any to the residue of my estate, or hold such articles or any of them until my child is old enough to make use of them.

I authorize my Estate Trustee to deliver any articles to my children at such times as my Estate Trustee considers appropriate, whether or not a child may be under the age of majority. The delivery of any articles to such child shall be a complete release to my Estate Trustee.

Any articles not distributed or retained shall become part of the residue of my estate.

Commentary: This precedent ensures that articles of personal property are available for the children, either by immediate gift or because the trustee will hold an article for a child until he or she is old enough to have it.

Beneficiaries under the age of majority (18 in Ontario) cannot give a valid receipt to a trustee for any asset distributed to them. This clause provides some discretion to the trustee to hold or sell articles or give them to the children even though they are underage.

As a practical matter, children who have lost their parents should have every opportunity to keep family articles, their own furniture, family heirlooms and any other article of real or sentimental value.

C-9 PERSONAL PROPERTY DIVIDED AMONG A GROUP.

Short description: This precedent provides for division of personal and household effects among a group.

PERSONAL PROPERTY

My Estate Trustee shall divide all articles of personal and household use or ornament among [my children] then living as they may agree, or failing agreement, as my Estate Trustee considers appropriate in the exercise of an absolute discretion. Any articles not chosen shall be sold and the proceeds added to the residue of my estate.

Commentary: This is a variation of earlier precedents. I generally use it for division among adult children or grandchildren.

I always invite the testator to consider whether these general clauses for distribution among the children will cause World War III. Often the answer is "Yes!", which leads to more complex drafting or to sending the testator away to make a memorandum which will be incorporated into the will (see precedent C-4).

C-10 DEBTS, DEATH TAXES AND CONVERSION OF ASSETS.

Short description: The trustee is directed to pay all debts and taxes payable in consequence of the testator's death. The trustee is directed to realize the assets of the estate and is not bound to rid the estate of those assets which are not "authorized" for trustees.

DEBTS AND DEATH TAXES

My Estate Trustee shall pay out of the capital of my estate all my just debts, including any income taxes payable for the year(s) prior to my death and in the year of my death to the date of my death, funeral and testamentary expenses, and all succession duties, estate, gift, inheritance and death taxes, whether imposed pursuant to the law of this or any other jurisdiction, otherwise payable by any beneficiary under my Will or any Codicil or of any settlement made by me, by any beneficiary named by me in any insurance policy, plan or contract owned by me, or by any donee of any gift made by me.

CONVERSION OF MY ASSETS

My Estate Trustee shall call in the assets of my estate and may sell the assets at such times, for such price, in such manner and upon such terms as my Estate Trustee in the exercise of an absolute discretion considers appropriate.

I authorize my Estate Trustee to hold any asset of my estate without liability for loss or depreciation for as long as my Estate Trustee in the exercise of an absolute discretion considers appropriate, whether or not it may not be an investment in which a trustee may by law invest trust funds.

Commentary: They say that death and taxes are the only certainties of life. By this clause, all debts incurred by the deceased in his or her lifetime, all funeral and testamentary expenses, all unpaid income taxes for any taxation year including the year of death, and any estate taxes or succession duties are to be paid out of the capital of the residue of the estate. It is possible to throw the tax burden onto the beneficiary who will receive a particular property such as the cottage or an RRSP. If that is to be the case, then this clause should be amended to exclude the specific property.

Section 5 of the *Estates Administration Act*, R.S.O. 1990, c. E.22, provides that:

> 5. Subject to section 32 of the *Succession Law Reform Act*, the real and personal property of a deceased person comprised in a residuary devise or bequest, except so far as a contrary intention appears from the person's will . . . is applicable rateably, according to their respective values, to the payment of his of her debts, funeral and testamentary expenses and the cost and expenses of administration.

Section 32 of the *Succession Law Reform Act* creates an important exception to this section: in the absence of an expressed contrary intention, a beneficiary of real property is liable for any mortgage on the property.

C-11 RESIDENCE HELD FOR USE BY NAMED BENEFICIARY.

Short description: Under this clause, the family home will be held to provide accommodation for a surviving spouse or other beneficiary. Expenses of maintaining the property are to be paid by whomever the testator directs. The home may be sold and a substitute residence bought or the cash proceeds of the sale added to the residue.

RESIDENCE

1. If my [husband] survives me, my Estate Trustees shall hold the real property which my [husband] and I are using as a principal residence (now referred to as "the Property") at the date of my death as a home for my [husband] and any one or more of my children until the "Disposition Date" which is the first to happen of:

(a) the date of my [husband's] death;
(b) the date upon which my [husband] notifies my Estate Trustees that [he] no longer wishes to have the Property held for [him];
(c) the date when my Estate Trustees consider it no longer appropriate to retain the Property as a home for my [husband], by reason of any illness, or for any other reason they in their absolute discretion determine.

Until the Disposition Date, the taxes, insurance, repairs, mortgage, and any other charges or amounts necessary for the general upkeep of the Property held under the terms of this paragraph shall be paid by my [husband].

Subject to the next paragraph of my Will, on the Disposition Date, my Estate Trustees shall sell the Property and add the proceeds of sale [*specify*].

Substituted Property

2. Prior to the Disposition Date, if my [husband] requests it of my Estate Trustees and my Estate Trustees in the exercise of an absolute discretion consider it appropriate prior to the distribution of the proceeds of sale of the Property, my Estate Trustees may use some or all of the proceeds to purchase or build another property of any kind, including a single family dwelling, a condominium unit, or an interest in a co-operative apartment (which shall be deemed to be "the Property" for all purposes of my Will) for the use of my [husband] as a residence, and so on from time to time. Any proceeds of sale not required for the purchase of such substitute property shall be added to [*specify*].

Commentary: Note that the testator may choose who will pay the expenses of keeping a residence on behalf of a named beneficiary. It is simplest to make the tenant pay; however, it gets difficult for the trustee if the tenant refuses to pay as there is no enforcement mechanism.

The testator may elect to have the estate pay the expenses. In this case, he or she should ensure that there is a fund from which expenses can be paid. A sample clause to create such a fund is found in precedent C-12. If the beneficiary is to pay the expenses, consider whether the mortgage is an appropriate expense.

A residence maintained for the surviving spouse qualifies the house as a principal residence for tax purposes: see s. 40(4) of the *Income Tax Act* (Canada) and Revenue Canada Interpretation Bulletin IT399R.

This clause contains a second provision concerning property held — that it can be sold and a substitute purchased in the discretion of the trustee or because the spouse or tenant wants it. The power to sell and substitute other accommodation is important. I have often seen a direction to hold a house until the death of a spouse with no other provision made, and the house or the neighbourhood deteriorates, or the spouse becomes too frail or too sick to stay in the house. Under such circumstances, the trustee should have the power to avoid having to hold the house.

If a less expensive substitute property is purchased, there will be an excess of proceeds over the purchase price of the new property. Remember to include a disposition of that amount. For example, the excess could be held in trust for the benefit of the tenant of the property, used to pay taxes and other expenses, or added to the residue of the estate.

C-12 HOUSE FUND TO MAINTAIN RESIDENCE IN TRUST.

Short description: This is a suitable clause for creating a fund to pay expenses for a house or cottage held in trust.

<u>HOUSE FUND</u>

My Estate Trustee shall set aside a sum of money which in [his *or* her] absolute discretion is sufficient to pay the taxes, insurance, repairs, mortgage and any other amount for the general upkeep of the residence. Such sum so set aside shall be referred to as the "House Fund" and shall be held on the following terms:

1. The expenses shall be paid out of income from the House Fund or out of the capital as my Estate Trustee in the exercise of an absolute discretion considers appropriate.
2. Any income not used in any year shall be accumulated and added to the capital of the House Fund.

3. If the House Fund is not sufficient to pay the expenses, my Estate Trustee in the exercise of an absolute discretion [*specify what trustee may do, such as mortgage or sell property*].
4. [*Specify final distribution if there is any House Fund left at the end of the trust for the residence.*]

Commentary: If the estate will pay the expenses of a residence held in trust, it is essential to ensure that there is a fund from which those expenses can be paid. Too many wills create a house or cottage trust and then give the residue outright. This creates an impossible situation for the trustee.

C-13 COTTAGE PROPERTY TO BE SOLD — OPTION TO NAMED BENEFICIARIES.

Short description: This clause allows a sale of cottage property at fair market value to a named beneficiary, and if that beneficiary does not want the cottage, there is provision for offering the cottage to others in order of age.

COTTAGE PROPERTY

If the cottage and property or any interest or rights with respect to such cottage or property are owned by me at the date of my death (now referred to in my Will as the "cottage"), my Estate Trustee shall allow   if [he *or* she] so wishes, to purchase the cottage from my estate at its fair market value.

The fair market value of the cottage shall be determined by my Estate Trustee whose decision as to the fair market value shall be binding on all beneficiaries of my estate.

          shall have ninety days from the date of my death to enter an enforceable agreement to purchase the cottage on the terms above set out. Failing agreement within ninety days, the rights to purchase the same given to   shall be null and void.

If   purchases the cottage, all expenses related to its transfer to   , including all solicitors' costs and any taxes, shall be borne by   .

If   does not wish to purchase the cottage, [my children], one at a time according to age from eldest to youngest, shall be given the opportunity to purchase the cottage on the same terms and conditions set forth above as   was given.

The cottage shall be offered to [my children], in the order above referred to, each to be given thirty days from the date of a notice by my Estate Trustee of the right to purchase the cottage, to enter an enforceable agreement to purchase the same on the terms above set forth. Failing agreement within thirty days, the right to purchase given shall be null and void.

The next in line shall be given the right to purchase on the terms above set out, and so on from time to time.

If a [child] fails to complete the purchase of the cottage which he or she has agreed to purchase in accordance with the terms above set out within a reasonable time, such time to be determined by my Estate Trustee in the exercise of an absolute discretion, the right to purchase given to such [child] shall be null and void.

If no [child of mine] purchases the cottage as above provided, such cottage shall fall into and form part of the residue of my estate.

Commentary: The family cottage is an asset for which careful planning is required since its distribution is often charged with years of emotional attachment. Holding the cottage in trust for all the children, who of course come with their own spouses and families, might create more difficulties than it will solve. This precedent demonstrates how a sale might be arranged. Where, however, a trust may suit the family's needs and dynamics better, a clause such as precedent C-14 could be used. Finally, a seasonal residence may be transferred outright to a family member. In a case such as this, it may be appropriate to charge that member with the tax consequence of the property rather than allowing the tax burden to be borne by the residuary beneficiaries.

C-14 COTTAGE TRUST.

Short description: This clause directs that the cottage be held until the death of the survivor of a class of beneficiaries and that the expenses of the cottage be paid by a specified group.

COTTAGE TRUST

My Estate Trustee shall hold the real property which I own and in which I have any interest and which I am using as a [summer home, ski chalet, etc.] at my death, which is located at . I will refer to such property as the "cottage". My Estate Trustee shall hold the cottage until the last to die of my [children] or for such shorter period as my Estate Trustee in the exercise of an absolute discretion considers appropriate.

The taxes, insurance, repairs, [mortgage] and any other expenses for the upkeep of the cottage shall be paid by .

[*Create rules for use by the children and their families, such as the period during which a child and his or her family can use the property, or simply leave a memorandum of "wishes" and let the children settle the use and payment of expenses among themselves.*]

Upon the death of my last surviving [child], or upon

the date when my Estate Trustee considers it no longer appropriate to retain the cottage, my Estate Trustee shall [*specify, for example, a division of the proceeds of sale among the issue of the testator equally per stirpes*].

Commentary: It is likely appropriate to direct that articles of household use, boats and accessories be held for use with the cottage.

See precedent C-11 for clauses suitable for holding real property in trust.

C-15 CASH LEGACIES.

Short description: Gifts of cash are made to named beneficiaries.

CASH LEGACIES

My Estate Trustee shall pay the following cash legacies as soon as possible after my death:

(a) to , the sum of $ if [he *or* she] survives me;

(b) to , the sum of $ if [he *or* she] survives me; and

(c) to , the sum of $ if [he *or* she] survives me.

Commentary: There are many variations of cash legacies. This precedent is the most typical. The testator may specify that a legacy is to be paid out of a particular fund or out of the proceeds of sale of a property. Such legacies, however, create interpretation problems where the fund has disappeared or the proceeds of sale are insufficient to pay all the legacies.

Cash legacies for minors sometimes create difficulties since the testator probably does not want the legacy managed by the court during the child's minority. One possible solution is to direct that the legacy be paid to the parent or guardian of the minor or to a trusted third party, coupled with the wish that the funds be used for the support and education of the minor. A second possibility, though likely a more expensive choice, would be to have the trustee continue to hold the legacy until the minor is 18 (or to a later date in appropriate circumstances). Precedents E-1 to E-6 are suitable for such trusts.

An estate which created much litigation and stated much law in the area of cash legacies and the distribution of specific property to the beneficiaries is *Millar (Re)*, [1927] 3 D.L.R. 270, 60 O.L.R. 434 (H.C.). The will in this case was the one which created the great baby derby of the 1930s and many other outrageous distributions.

C-16 CHARITABLE BEQUEST.

Short description: A cash legacy is paid to a named charity. The trustee is discharged by obtaining a receipt from the organization. The trustee is not required to see that the charitable purpose is carried out.

CHARITABLE BEQUEST

My Estate Trustee shall pay to the sum of $. The receipt of the treasurer or other proper officer of this organization shall be a sufficient discharge to my Estate Trustee.

Commentary: A gift for a purpose is not valid unless that purpose is charitable. The following have been identified as charitable purposes: the advancement of religion, the advancement of education, relief of poverty and public benefit.

As a practical matter, there are numerous cases where the charity of choice is improperly described or does not exist at the date of the testator's death. If there is no successor to a charity no longer in existence, the court will attempt to discover the intention of the testator, and, if the chosen charity has an overriding general charitable purpose, then the court will substitute a charity with a similar purpose.

Then there is the problem of a charity being improperly described. More diligent investigation by the solicitor drafting the will could save a particular gift. For example, to ensure the charity is correctly named, there are many directories of charitable organizations available, and a quick telephone call to a proposed charity will usually turn up the needed information.

See A.H. Oosterhoff and E.E. Gillese, *Text, Commentary and Cases on Trusts*, 4th ed. (Toronto, Carswell, 1992), Chapter 15, Part 7, for a discussion of how the courts will attempt to save otherwise failed charitable bequests. See Chapter 16 of the same publication for a discussion of trusts with non-charitable purposes.

D. OUTRIGHT DISTRIBUTIONS OF RESIDUE

These are the most straightforward precedents in the book and are always appropriate where the beneficiary is capable and responsible, and where the estate is of average value and complexity and in no great need of significant tax planning.

There are several matters to take into account:

1. The survivorship period. You will see reference in many of the clauses to the requirement that the beneficiary, usually the spouse, in order to inherit, must be alive 30 days after the date of death. Refer to the commentary and annotations to precedent D-1.

2. Avoiding the use of the following incorrect distribution clauses (these are the common errors of inexperienced drafters):

   (a) "To divide the residue of my estate among my *children* in equal shares *per stirpes*". Such a distribution is technically impossible because of the meaning of a *per stirpes* distribution which requires a common root. It is correct to direct the division to be "among my *issue* in equal shares *per stirpes*".

   (b) "To pay the residue to my husband and after his death to pay it to our children in equal shares". You cannot graft a life interest onto an outright distribution.

   (c) "To pay the residue to Mr. and Mrs.   ". What if only one survives? Also, try to name the beneficiaries individually rather than as set out here.

D-1 RESIDUE OUTRIGHT TO SPOUSE.

Short description: The residue of the estate is directed to be paid to the spouse if he or she survives for 30 days.

RESIDUE

If [my husband], , is living on the thirtieth day following the date of my death, my Estate Trustee shall pay and transfer the residue of my estate to [him] for [his] own use absolutely.

Commentary: This is the most typical distribution of estates of average complexity and value. Generally the wills of husbands and wives are identical to each other ("mirror wills"), providing that the surviving spouse will be the sole executor and sole beneficiary (with some minor variations).

Note the survivorship requirement of 30 days. Another version of such a requirement is the "quick succession" clause which refers to the circumstance of two people, usually spouses, dying where it is not possible to state which one survived the other. An obvious example is an airline disaster where no survivors are found. However, if there is evidence of survivorship even for, say, two hours, then the whole estate of the one spouse will pass to the one who survives and be immediately distributable out of the estate of the survivor. This is clearly an unfortunate result, since it can involve double estate administration, double fees and often double tax. I much prefer the 30-day provision.

It is within the context of the survivorship clause that one of the most common drafting errors occurs: the will provides for a distribution if the spouse predeceases or dies within the 30-day period but does not provide for the spouse surviving the 30-day period. The result is an application under rule 14.05(3)[5] of the Rules of Civil Procedure to invite the court to supply the missing distribution, but the decisions are very uneven. *R. v. Craig* (1978), 149 D.L.R. (3d) 483, 42 O.R. (2d) 567 (C.A.), takes a hard line on supplying the missing distribution; *Harmer (Re)* (1964), 46 D.L.R. (2d) 521, [1965] S.C.R. 24 *sub nom. Kilby v. Myers*, provides a more relaxed view of the court's ability to find and supply the missing distribution; and there are many other cases on both sides of the issue.

[5] Amended O. Reg. 396/91, s. 3.

Part IV of the *Succession Law Reform Act* addresses the issue of survivorship if the will has not done so. Where two or more persons die at the same time or it is uncertain who died first, each is deemed to have survived the other. The result is that the alternative distributions created by the will take effect, or, on an intestacy, the nearest surviving kin will inherit (see Part II of the *Succession Law Reform Act* for a description of the intestacy provisions). Part IV also addresses the issue of the simultaneous death of joint tenants, deeming each to have survived the other.

D-2 RESIDUE OUTRIGHT TO NAMED BENEFICIARY; GIFT OVER TO SUBSTITUTES IN SUCCESSION.

Short description: This is an outright gift of the residue to a named beneficiary provided that the named beneficiary survives the deceased by 30 days. There is a gift over to a substitute beneficiary if the named beneficiary fails to survive and a second alternative gift over to a third named beneficiary in the same circumstances.

RESIDUE

If   is living on the thirtieth day following my death, my Estate Trustee shall pay and transfer the residue of my estate to   . If   is not then living, my Estate Trustee shall pay and transfer the residue to   . If   is not then living, my Estate Trustee shall pay and transfer the residue to   .

Commentary: This is a variation of precedent D-1 which addresses some of the drafting problems mentioned in the commentary at the beginning of this section.

D-3 RESIDUE DIVIDED EQUALLY AMONG NAMED BENEFICIARIES; GIFTS OVER TO ISSUE.

Short description: This is a division of the residue among named beneficiaries. If a named beneficiary predeceases, his or her issue will take equally *per stirpes*.

RESIDUE

My Estate Trustee shall divide the residue of my estate into two equal parts and shall deal with such parts as follows:

(a) One part shall be paid and transferred to , if is living at the date of my death. If is not then living, such part shall be divided in equal shares *per stirpes* among 's issue then living.

(b) One part shall be paid and transferred to , if is living at the date of my death. If is not then living, such part shall be divided in equal shares *per stirpes* among 's issue then living.

Commentary: This clause is typically used for distribution of residue between (or, if more than two, among) the children of the deceased. It is often the alternative distribution to follow precedent D-1, in which case precedent D-1 says: "If is not living on the thirtieth day following the date of my death, my Estate Trustee shall divide . . .".

Note that this clause assumes named beneficiaries have issue, which may be inappropriate (see precedent D-4).

D-4 RESIDUE DIVIDED EQUALLY AMONG NAMED BENEFICIARIES; GIFTS OVER TO ISSUE.

Short description: This clause directs a division of the residue among named beneficiaries. If a named beneficiary predeceases, there is a gift over to his or her issue in equal shares *per stirpes*. If there is no issue, the equal share accrues to the surviving child or to his or her issue as the case may be.

RESIDUE

My Estate Trustee shall divide the residue of my estate equally between [my son], , and [my daughter], . If either of my children is not living at the date of my death but leaves issue then living, the share of the residue of my estate to which such child would have been entitled if living shall be divided among the issue then living of such child in equal shares *per stirpes*.

If either child is not then living and leaves no issue then living, the share of the residue of my estate to which such child could have been entitled if living shall be paid to the survivor of my children.

Commentary: This clause addresses the problem, mentioned in precedent D-3, of named beneficiaries having no children.

D-5 ALTERNATIVE RESIDUE TO DECEASED'S ISSUE IF NAMED BENEFICIARY DOES NOT SURVIVE.

Short description: If a named beneficiary is not living on the thirtieth day following the date of death of the testator, the residue is to be divided among the deceased's issue in equal shares *per stirpes*.

ALTERNATIVE RESIDUE

If   is not living on the thirtieth day following my death, my Estate Trustee shall divide the residue of my estate among my issue then living in equal shares *per stirpes*.

Commentary: This clause is the most typical alternative to the distribution provided for in precedent D-1. It is appropriate where the children (*i.e.*, the first generation) are adults who do not need trusts created for their interests in the estate because they are mature and responsible — or never will be.

If the estate is sufficiently large, a testator may want to create trusts for his or her children and minor grandchildren which extend the distributions beyond age 18. The precedents in the next section, "Trust Clauses", are pertinent to this situation.

D-6 EQUAL DIVISION AMONG A GROUP.

Short description: The estate trustee is directed to provide an equal share for each of the survivors or several named persons or a class of persons.

RESIDUE IN EQUAL SHARES

My Estate Trustee shall divide the residue of my estate into the number of equal shares required to effect the following distribution:

(a) One equal share shall be paid to , or if [he] does not survive me, shall be divided among [his] children equally *per capita*, subject to paragraph of my Will (which provides for my nieces and nephews).

(b) One equal share shall be paid to , or if [he] does not survive me, shall be divided among [his] children equally *per capita*, subject to paragraph of my Will (which provides for my nieces and nephews).

(c) One equal share shall be paid to if [she] survives me.

(d) One equal share shall be paid to each child of who survives me, subject to paragraph of my Will (which provides for such children).

Commentary: This clause is often used for gifts to unrelated people. Each person is to receive an equal gift, but only if he or she survives the testator.

E. TRUST CLAUSES

Plain, concise language is critical throughout the will but is most important when setting up trusts. We have all seen trust clauses which run on and on, separated by semicolons, and which are all but impossible to follow. Is it any wonder that drafting errors result?

A main error in establishing trusts is assuming that all the beneficiaries will die in the right order — life tenant first after the testator, then the children, then the grandchildren, all inheriting as adults. However, the will should plan for other reasonably possible contingencies.

One question that needs to be asked of your client is how old the children ought to be in order to inherit. While there are young financial Einsteins out there, most children are much too young at age 18 to inherit an estate, with the chances excellent that at age 18½, the money will have evaporated. The same pertains to the grandchildren. They will not be any more ready at 18 than their parents would have been. The obvious answer is to postpone the distribution until a later age. If the estate is reasonably large, I recommend that money be paid out in several instalments of the capital to ensure that, if the first lot is wasted, at least the child may have learned something by the time of the second distribution.

A second question that needs to be asked is how long to keep the money in trust. In my view, until the child reaches age 30 or 35 is long enough. If a child is irresponsible at 35, he or she will probably be irresponsible at 40 or 45 and so on.

Finally, there is much scope for tax planning with the residue of sufficiently large estates. The February, 1995, federal budget removed what was a valuable ability to have income allocated to a beneficiary without actually paying the income to him or her. The income would then be taxed in the hands of the beneficiary at lower rates than would be paid by the trust. Many trusts drafted before February, 1995, were drafted to take advantage of that provision. Now income must be paid to the beneficiary in order to have an income inclusion in the beneficiary's hands and a deduction to the trust.

There are many non-tax reasons for trusts, and therefore, many versions of trusts. The reader is advised to consult other precedent books such as *O'Brien's Encyclopedia of Forms*, 11th ed., Division V, Wills and Trusts (Aurora, Canada Law Book, 1993, looseleaf) and to work closely with trust and tax lawyers, tax accountants and other professionals with pertinent experience.

E-1 TRUSTS FOR CHILDREN AND ISSUE OF DECEASED ISSUE — ONE CAPITAL DISTRIBUTION.

Short description: This clause provides for a division among living children and the issue of deceased children. There is one capital distribution at a specific age for each child. Prior to that time, the trustee has full discretion to encroach on income and capital for support and education. There is gift over of a child's share.

CHILDREN'S PROVISIONS

[If   is not living on the thirtieth day following my death,] my Estate Trustee shall divide the residue of my estate so that there is:

(a) one equal part for each child of mine living at the death of the survivor of   and me, and

(b) one equal part for each child of mine not then living with issue then living.

My Estate Trustee shall deal with such parts as follows:

(a) (i) My Estate Trustee shall set aside one part for each child then living and shall keep the part invested. Until my child attains age   , my Estate Trustee shall pay to him or her or apply to his or her support and education so much of the income and capital of the part as my Estate Trustee in the exercise of an absolute discretion considers appropriate from time to time. Any surplus income shall be accumulated and added to the part.

(ii) When my child attains age   , my Estate Trustee shall transfer the balance of the part to him or her.

(b) (i) If my child dies before attaining age   , my Estate Trustee shall divide the part or the amount not yet received by my child, equally [*per capita*] among the [children] of my child who survive him or her. If my child leaves no child surviving him or her, the part shall be divided among my issue alive at the death of my child in equal shares *per stirpes*.

(ii) If, however, an interest passes to any child of mine for whom a part of my estate is being held in trust under my Will, that interest shall be added to the trust for the child of mine and shall be administered in the same manner.

(c) My Estate Trustee shall set aside one part for the issue of each child of mine not living on the thirtieth day following my death, but who has issue then living, and shall divide the part among the then living issue of such child in equal shares *per stirpes*.

Commentary: This clause, with one capital distribution, is suitable for estates of modest complexity and size.

As mentioned in the commentary to this section, it is usually appropriate to extend a child's distribution beyond the age of majority. Most testators understand this, but are concerned to ensure that their children are properly educated and cared for in a way they would have been had the testator lived.

Subparagraph (c) sometimes confuses first-time drafters. It provides for a distribution to grandchildren where a child is not living on the thirtieth day following the death of the testator. Subparagraph (b), on the other hand, addresses a gift for grandchildren where the child has survived the thirtieth day but dies before the age of final distribution.

Subparagraph (b)(i) provides for an equal distribution to the grandchildren when the specified child of the testator dies before the trust is terminated. I usually restrict this distribution to the next generation only, unless the estate is very large or the age of final distribution is postponed beyond age 40, when it is possible that there will be grandchildren of a deceased child. This is, of course, very remote.

E-2 TRUSTS FOR CHILDREN AND ISSUE OF DECEASED ISSUE — TWO CAPITAL DISTRIBUTIONS.

Short description: This clause provides for a division of the residue equally among surviving children and the issue of deceased children. A share for each child is held in trust. Income and capital are to be paid at the discretion of the trustee to the child or for the support and education of the child until the first capital distribution. Income is then paid directly to the child until the final distribution, when the whole of the share is transferred to the child.

CHILDREN'S PROVISIONS

[If   is not living on the thirtieth day following my death,] my Estate Trustee shall divide the residue of my estate so that there is:

(a) one equal part for each child of mine living at the death of the survivor of   and me, and

(b) one equal part for each child of mine not then living with issue then living.

My Estate Trustee shall deal with such parts as follows:

(a) (i) My Estate Trustee shall set aside one part for each child then living and shall keep the part invested. Until my child attains age   , my Estate Trustee shall pay to him or her or apply to his or her support and education so much of the income and capital of the part as my Estate Trustee in the exercise of an absolute discretion considers appropriate from time to time. Any surplus income shall be accumulated and added to the part.

(ii) When my child attains age   , my Estate Trustee shall transfer [one-half] of the amount of the part then remaining to him or her.

(iii) Thereafter my Estate Trustee shall pay the net income derived from the part to my child together with so much of the capital as my Estate Trustee in the exercise of an absolute discretion considers appropriate from time to time for his or her support and education.

(iv) When my child attains age , my Estate Trustee shall transfer the balance of the part to him or her.

(b) (i) If my child dies before attaining age , my Estate Trustee shall divide the part or the amount not yet received by my child, equally [*per capita*] among the [children] of my child who survive him or her. If my child leaves no child surviving him or her, the part shall be divided among my issue alive at the death of my child in equal shares *per stirpes.*

(ii) If, however, an interest passes to any child of mine for whom a part of my estate is being held in trust under my Will, that interest shall be added to the trust for the child of mine and shall be administered in the same manner.

(iii) My Estate Trustee shall set aside one part for the issue of each child of mine not living on the thirtieth day following my death, but who has issue then living, and shall divide the part among the then living issue of such child in equal shares *per stirpes*.

Commentary: This clause is a variation of precedent E-1 and creates a staged distribution for children. The purpose of the first distribution is to give the child an opportunity to experience ownership of a capital amount, including not using the capital wisely. However, if the child does misuse this part of his or her inheritance, perhaps something will have been learned by the time of the second distribution, and the bulk of the estate will thereby be protected.

E-3 TRUSTS FOR CHILDREN AND ISSUE OF DECEASED ISSUE — THREE CAPITAL DISTRIBUTIONS.

Short description: This clause provides for three capital distributions. Until the first distribution, income and capital may be paid for the benefit of the child. After the first capital distribution, the child is entitled to all of the income and to encroachments at the discretion of the trustee.

TRUSTS FOR CHILDREN

[If   is not living on the thirtieth day following my death,] my Estate Trustee shall divide the residue of my estate so that there is:

(a) one equal part for each child of mine living at the death of the survivor of   and me, and
(b) one equal part for each child of mine not then living with issue then living.

My Estate Trustee shall deal with such parts as follows:

(a) (i) My Estate Trustee shall set aside one part for each child then living and shall keep the part invested. Until my child attains age   , my Estate Trustee shall pay to him or her or apply to his or her support and education so much of the income and capital of the part as my Estate Trustee in the exercise of an absolute discretion considers appropriate from time to time. Any surplus income shall be accumulated and added to the part.

(ii) Thereafter my Estate Trustee shall pay the net income to my child, until he or she attains age   .

(iii) When my child attains age   , my Estate Trustee shall pay and transfer [one-third] of the part then remaining to my child for his or her own use absolutely.

(iv) Thereafter my Estate Trustee shall pay the net income to my child until he or she attains age .

(v) When my child attains age , my Estate Trustee shall pay and transfer [one-half] of the part then remaining to my child for his or her own use absolutely.

(vi) Thereafter my Estate Trustee shall pay the net income to my child until he or she attains age .

(vii) At any time my Estate Trustee may pay to or for my child such amounts out of the capital of the part as my Estate Trustee in the exercise of an absolute discretion considers appropriate for the support and education of my child.

(viii) When my child attains age , my Estate Trustee shall transfer the balance of the part to my child for his or her own use absolutely.

(b) (i) If my child dies before attaining age , my Estate Trustee shall divide the part or the amount not yet received by my child, equally [*per capita*] among the [children] of my child who survive him or her. If my child leaves no child surviving him or her, the part shall be divided among my issue alive at the death of my child in equal shares *per stirpes*.

(ii) If, however, an interest passes to any child of mine for whom a part of my estate is being held in trust under my Will, that interest shall be added to such trust and be administered as if an original portion of it.

(c) My Estate Trustee shall set aside one part for the issue of each child of mine not living at my death, but who has issue then living, and shall divide the part among the then living issue of such child in equal shares *per stirpes*.

Commentary: This is another variation of precedent E-1 and provides for three capital distributions. This is a typical distribution to children where the estate is very large. It is useful to discuss with the testator the choice of ages for the capital distributions. Testators have different views on the length of time funds should be held in trust for their children.

E-4 POOL OF RESIDUE FOR CHILDREN.

Short description: This clause creates a pool of the residue for the benefit of all the children. The trustees have full discretion to encroach upon income and capital for any of the children and may choose to exclude a child.

RESIDUE — TRUSTS FOR CHILDREN

If my [wife] is not living on the thirtieth day following the date of my death, my Estate Trustee shall set aside the residue of my estate upon trust on the following terms:

(a) Until my eldest living child attains age , my Estate Trustee shall pay to my children or either of them such amounts out of the income and capital of the residue of my estate to or for the support and education of my children or either of them, all as my Estate Trustee in the exercise of an absolute discretion considers appropriate.

(b) When my eldest living child attains age , or on the date of my death if that occurs first, my Estate Trustee shall divide the residue of my estate in the following manner:

[(i) I declare that any amounts which my Estate Trustee has paid to or for a child of mine out of the capital of the residue of my estate, pursuant to paragraph

(a) of my Will, shall be brought into account in the division of the residue of my estate as against such child and his or her issue.

(ii) Subject to the adjustment directed by paragraph (b)(i) of my Will, my Estate Trustee shall divide the residue then remaining so that there is one equal part for each child of mine then living, and one equal part for each child of mine not then living with issue then living. My Estate Trustee shall deal with such parts as follows:]

My Estate Trustee shall pay one part to each child of mine who has attained age .

My Estate Trustee shall set aside one part for each child then living and under age and shall keep the part invested. Until my child atttains age , my Estate Trustee shall pay to him or her or apply to his or her support and education so much of the income and capital of the part as my Estate Trustee in the exercise of an absolute discretion considers appropriate from time to time. Any surplus income shall be accumulated and added to the part.

When my child attains age , my Estate Trustee shall transfer the balance of the part to him or her.

If my child dies before attaining age , my Estate Trustee shall divide the part or the amount not yet received by my child, equally [*per capita*] among the [children] of my child who survive him or her. If my child leaves no child surviving him or her, the part shall be divided among my issue alive at the death of my child in equal shares *per stirpes*.

If, however, an interest passes to any child of mine for whom a part of my estate is being held in trust under my Will, that interest shall be added to the trust for the child of mine and shall be administered in the same manner.

> My Estate Trustee shall set aside one part for the issue of each child of mine not living at the date of death of the survivor of [my wife] and me, but who has issue then living, and shall divide the part among the then living issue of such child in equal shares *per stirpes*.

Commentary: This clause is particularly useful when there is a great spread of years between the children. The testator may have already paid for all the education of the older children but not for the education of a younger child. It would be unfair to divide the estate equally, as was the case in precedents E-1 to E-3, because the younger child would have to bear the cost of education out of his or her trust fund while the others would have theirs to do with as they saw fit.

The *Accumulations Act*, R.S.O. 1990, c. A.5, s. 1(1), limits the length of time during which trustees may capitalize income which is not paid out. For our purposes, the important period occurs on the twenty-first anniversary of the testator's death. After that date, the income must be paid out and if there is no direction as to how that should happen, then there will be an intestacy and it will be a question of will interpretation as to who the beneficiaries of the income ought to be: see *Martin (Re)* (1979), 98 D.L.R. (3d) 570, 24 O.R. (2d) 408 (C.A.).

E-5 SPECIAL PROVISIONS FOR GRANDCHILDREN — ONE CAPITAL DISTRIBUTION.

Short description: Special trusts are to be created for the interests of each grandchild who is under a specified age. Until a grandchild attains that age, the trustee has full discretion to encroach upon income and capital for his or her support and education. There is only one capital distribution.

Special Provisions for my Grandchildren

If, as the result of the distributions provided for in my Will, a grandchild of mine becomes entitled to receive any amount out of the capital of the residue of my estate before attaining age , the amount (referred to as "the part") shall be held and invested by my Estate Trustee upon the following terms:

(a) (i) Until such grandchild attains age , my Estate Trustee shall pay to him or her or apply to his or her support and education so much of the income and capital of the part as my Estate Trustee in the exercise of an absolute discretion considers appropriate from time to time. Any surplus income shall be accumulated and added to the part.

(ii) When such grandchild attains age , my Estate Trustee shall transfer the balance of the part to him or her.

(b) (i) If a grandchild dies before attaining age , my Estate Trustee shall divide the part or the amount not yet received by such grandchild, equally [*per capita*] among the [children] of such grandchild who survive him or her. If such grandchild leaves no child surviving him or her, the part shall be divided among [my issue] alive at the death of my child in equal shares [*per stirpes*].

Commentary: This clause is appropriate in the case of a small to moderate-sized trust. For a similar clause where a larger estate is involved, see precedent E-6.

E-6 SPECIAL PROVISIONS FOR GRANDCHILDREN — TWO CAPITAL DISTRIBUTIONS.

Short description: This clause provides for the interests of the grandchildren to be held in separate trusts and for two capital distributions. Until the final capital distribution, the grandchild is entitled to one advance of capital and to income and other capital advances at the discretion of the trustee.

SPECIAL PROVISIONS FOR MY GRANDCHILDREN

If, as the result of the distributions provided for in my Will, a grandchild of mine becomes entitled to receive any amount out of the capital of the residue of my estate before attaining age , the amount (referred to as "the part") shall be held and invested by my Estate Trustee upon the following terms:

(a) (i) Until such grandchild attains age , my Estate Trustee shall pay to him or her or apply to his or her support and education so much of the income and capital of the part as my Estate Trustee in the exercise of an absolute discretion considers appropriate from time to time. Any surplus income shall be accumulated and added to the part.

(ii) When such grandchild attains age , my Estate Trustee shall transfer [one-half] of the part then remaining to him or her.

(iii) Thereafter my Estate Trustee shall pay to or for such grandchild so much of the income and capital of the part as my Estate Trustee in the exercise of an absolute discretion considers appropriate for his or her support and education.

(iv) When such grandchild attains age , my Estate Trustee shall transfer the balance of the part to him or her.

(b) If a grandchild dies before attaining age , my Estate Trustee shall divide the part or the amount not yet received by such grandchild, equally [*per capita*] among the [children] of such grandchild who survive him or her. If such grandchild leaves no child surviving him or her, the part shall be divided among [my issue] alive at the death of my child in equal shares [*per stirpes*].

Commentary: Provisions for grandchildren are appropriate where interests in the estate are large and ought not to be transferred to the grandchildren when they attain age 18 on the theory that an 18-year-old is, generally speaking, not old enough to manage money.

This clause can be modified to provide for "any beneficiary".

E-7 SPOUSE TRUST.

Short description: The residue is held in trust for the lifetime of the surviving spouse. The spouse is entitled to all of the net income and to capital encroachments at the discretion of the trustee.

SPOUSE TRUST

My Estate Trustee shall hold the residue of my estate upon trust during the lifetime of my [wife], . My Estate Trustee shall pay the net income to my [wife] and may pay to or use for the support, maintenance and benefit of such amounts out of the capital as my Estate Trustee in the exercise of an absolute discretion considers appropriate from time to time.

Commentary: Spouse trusts are often used for the protection of the spouse and children of the testator. The clause ensures that the spouse will be maintained during his or her lifetime and that the residue of the estate will be kept reasonably intact for the children. This is often a very great concern of testators, especially where they perceive that their spouse may remarry and divert the estate to strangers.

One of the primary obligations of a trustee is to keep an even hand among the beneficiaries of a trust. Unless the trust document provides otherwise, the trustee must consider all of the competing interests in the trust on an equal footing. The precedent as it has been drafted here does not create a preference for the spouse. If a preference for the spouse is desirable, you might want to draft the precedent to state that the trustee need not keep an even hand between the spouse and the residuary beneficiaries of the trust, the interests of the spouse being paramount. See, however, *Schipper v. Guaranty Trust Co. of Canada* (1989), 69 O.R. (2d) 386, 35 O.A.C. 238 (C.A.).

The choice of trustees for the spouse trust is an important decision for the testator. The spouse could be the sole trustee; however, this creates a number of conflicts of interest which can be difficult for the spouse.

Here are two practice tips. First, watch out for this common drafting error: "If my spouse is living on the thirtieth day following my death, my Estate Trustee shall transfer the residue of my estate to [him *or* her] and on [his *or* her] death, my Estate Trustee shall divide the residue of my estate among my issue in equal shares *per stirpes*." Clearly you cannot couple an absolute gift to the spouse with a trust and there are many cases in which a will written in this way had to be interpreted.

The second practice tip is to remind you to include a final distribution of the estate after the death of the spouse or on the death of the testator if the spouse predeceases.

There are many cases where the testator has failed to create a distribution following the death of the spouse or in the event of the spouse predeceasing: see, for example, *Stork Estate v. Stork* (1990), 72 O.R. (2d) 625, 38 E.T.R. 290 (H.C.J.). In that case, the only event which was not provided for in the will was the event that actually occurred. You will avoid this kind of drafting if the clause which next follows the creation of the spouse trust says: "Upon the death of my spouse, or upon my death if my spouse predeceases me . . .".

Section 70(6)[6] of the *Income Tax Act* of Canada has tax rules for

[6] Amended 1994, c. 7, Sch. II, s. 48(2), (3); *idem*, Sch. VIII, s. 28(4) to (6); 1994, c. 21, s. 33(6), (7).

distributions to spouses and spouse trusts. These rules provide, generally speaking, that when property is left to a spouse directly or through a spouse trust, the property of the deceased is *not* deemed disposed of immediately before death and therefore the capital gains consequences can be deferred until actual disposition of the property or until the death of the surviving spouse. This may create a substantial tax saving for the estate. In order for the deferrals to occur in the context of a spouse trust, no person other than the spouse can receive income or capital from the trust during the lifetime of the spouse. You are referred to Interpretation Bulletins IT-305R3, IT-449R and IT-207R. These interpretation bulletins are of great assistance in determining whether, for tax purposes, a spouse trust has been established.

The Ontario *Family Law Act*, s. 6, provides that the surviving spouse may elect between the benefits created for him or her by the *Family Law Act* and the benefits given by the will. It is essential to advise the testator that the spouse is able to elect against the spouse trust, thereby defeating this careful planning. There are a number of remedies. First, it would be useful to have the spouse be a party to any discussion about the spouse trust, how it might work and how it can be beneficial. Secondly, it is possible to have the spouses contract out of the ability to elect under the *Family Law Act*. The junior drafter is advised to consult family law and estate planning experts.

E-8 DIVISION INTO FAMILY TRUSTS.

Short description: The residue of the estate is divided into equal shares for each living child. Each share will be held in trust until the death of that child (or the trustee may have discretion to terminate the trust earlier if there is no good tax or personal reason to continue to hold the share in trust). In the meantime, the trustee has full discretion to "sprinkle" the income and capital among the child, his or her children and other issue and in some cases the child's spouse if the testator considers that advisable.

(For this precedent, names have been used to make it easier to follow.)

RESIDUE

On the death of the survivor of my husband and me, my Estate Trustee shall divide the residue of my estate into two (2) equal shares.

[Janet's] Trust

If my daughter, [Janet Smith], is then living, my Estate Trustee shall pay and transfer one equal share of the residue of my estate to the special Trustees now appointed in this paragraph, to be held by them upon the following terms:

(i) I appoint my daughter, [Janet Smith], and [John Brown] to be the special Trustees of one equal share of the residue of my estate (referred to as "[Janet's] Trust" in this paragraph). I will refer to the special Trustees of [Janet's] Trust as "[Janet's] Trustees".

(ii) [Janet's] Trustees shall have all the same powers, discretions and authorities as I have given to my Estate Trustee in my Will.

(iii) Until the Division Day (hereinafter defined), [Janet's] Trustees may pay to any one or more of my daughter, her husband, and her children, and to the exclusion of any one or more of them, for their support and benefit or education, such amounts out of the income derived from [Janet's] Trust and out of the capital thereof that in their absolute discretion [Janet's] Trustees consider appropriate from time to time.

(iv) After 21 years after the date of my death, [Janet's] Trustees shall divide the net income derived from [Janet's] Trust among any one or more of my daughter, her husband, and her children, and to the exclusion of any one or more of them, that in their absolute discretion [Janet's] Trustees consider appropriate from time to time.

Division Day

The "Division Day" of [Janet's] Trust shall be the first to happen of:

(a) the date prior to the date of death of my daughter, [Janet Smith], that [Janet's] Trustees select as the Division Day;

(b) the date of death of my daughter, [Janet Smith].

If [Janet's] Trustees have selected a date prior to the date of death of my daughter, [Janet's] Trustees shall pay and transfer [Janet's] Trust to my daughter, [Janet Smith], for her own use absolutely.

If the Division Day is the date of death of my daughter, [Janet Smith], [Janet's] Trustees shall dispose of [Janet's] Trust in such manner as my daughter, [Janet Smith], may by her last Will have appointed. In default of such appointment, or in so far as it does not take effect, [Janet's] Trust shall be divided among the issue of my daughter, [Janet Smith], in equal shares *per stirpes*, subject to [*paragraph dealing with shares of grandchildren*].

If my daughter leaves no issue then living, subject to [*paragraph dealing with shares of grandchildren*], [Janet's] Trust shall be added to [Robert's] Trust to follow the destination thereof.

[Janet] Not Living

If my daughter, [Janet Smith], is not living on the date of death of the survivor of my husband and me, [Janet's] Trustees shall dispose of [Janet's] Trust in such manner as my daughter, [Janet Smith], may by her last Will have appointed. In default of such appointment, or in so far as it does not take effect, [Janet's] Trust shall be divided among the issue of my daughter, [Janet Smith], in equal shares *per stirpes*, subject to [*paragraph dealing with shares of grandchildren*].

If my daughter leaves no issue then living, subject to [*paragraph dealing with shares of grandchildren*], [Janet's] Trust shall be added to [Robert's] Trust to follow the destination thereof.

[Robert's] Trust

If my son, [Robert Smith], is then living, my Estate Trustee shall pay and transfer one equal share of the residue of my estate to the special Trustees now appointed in this paragraph, to be held by them upon the following terms:

(i) I appoint my son, [Robert Smith], and [John Brown] to be the special Trustees of one equal share of the residue of my estate (referred to as "[Robert's] Trust" in this paragraph). I will refer to the special Trustees of [Robert's] Trust as "[Robert's] Trustees".

(ii) [Robert's] Trustees shall have all the same powers, discretions and authorities as I have given to my Estate Trustee in my Will.

(iii) Until the Division Day (hereinafter defined), [Robert's] Trustees may pay to any one or more of my son, his wife, and his children, and to the exclusion of any one or more of them, for their support and benefit, such amounts out of the income derived from [Robert's] Trust and out of the capital thereof that in their absolute discretion [Robert's] Trustees consider appropriate from time to time.

(iv) After 21 years after the date of my death, [Robert's] Trustees shall divide the net income derived from [Robert's] Trust among any one or more of my son, his wife, and his children, and to the exclusion of any one or more of them, that in their absolute discretion [Robert's] Trustees consider appropriate from time to time.

Division Day

The "Division Day" of [Robert's] Trust shall be the first to happen of:

(a) the date prior to the date of death of my son, [Robert Smith], that [Robert's] Trustees select as the Division Day;

(b) the date of death of my son, [Robert Smith].

If [Robert's] Trustees have selected a date prior to the date of death of my son, [Robert's] Trustees shall pay and transfer [Robert's] Trust to my son, [Robert Smith], for his own use absolutely.

If the Division Day is the date of death of my son, [Robert Smith], [Robert's] Trustees shall dispose of [Robert's] Trust in such manner as my son, [Robert Smith], may by his last Will have appointed. In default of such appointment, or in so far as it does not take effect, [Robert's] Trust shall be divided among the issue of my son, [Robert Smith], in equal shares *per stirpes*, subject to [*paragraph dealing with shares of grandchildren*].

If my son leaves no issue then living, subject to [*paragraph dealing with shares of grandchildren*], [Robert's] Trust shall be added to [Janet's] Trust to follow the destination thereof.

[Robert] Not Living

If my son, [Robert Smith], is not living on the date of death of the survivor of my husband and me, [Robert's] Trustees shall dispose of [Robert's] Trust in such manner as my son, [Robert Smith], may by his last Will have appointed. In default of such appointment, or in so far as it does not take effect, [Robert's] Trust shall be divided among the issue of my son, [Robert Smith], in equal shares *per stirpes*, subject to [*paragraph dealing with shares of grandchildren*].

If my son leaves no issue then living, subject to [*paragraph dealing with shares of grandchildren*], [Robert's] Trust shall be added to [Janet's] Trust to follow the destination thereof.

Commentary: This kind of planning can be very useful for wealthier families where the children have good incomes and would benefit by having expenses they would otherwise be paying out of after-tax income met out of the trust and taxed in the hands of the next generation.

It is recommended that the less experienced lawyer review the trust and tax considerations of such trusts with an estate and tax lawyer.

Note that it is generally advisable to ensure that the trustee can terminate the trust at his or her discretion to avoid having the family's interests tied up in a trust which is no longer tax efficient or is not suitable for the family's needs.

I have included "Special Trustees" for each trust, to ensure that the siblings are not trustees of each other's trusts. It is not appropriate in most circumstances for the siblings to be involved in each other's ongoing financial affairs.

Note that each of the children is given power to direct how his or her share will be disposed of if he or she dies. This is a good idea where the trusts will extend over a long period since "Janet" and "Robert" will have a much better idea than Grandma or Grandpa about how and when their own children should inherit.

E-9 FAMILY TRUST.

Short description: A named beneficiary such as the spouse is entitled to net income until his or her death. The trustee has full discretion to encroach upon capital not only for the benefit of the named beneficiary but also for the children of the testator. The trustee may choose to exclude any of those people from any distribution.

<u>FAMILY TRUST</u>

My Estate Trustee shall set aside the residue of my estate upon trust (hereinafter called the "Family Trust"). My Estate Trustee shall invest the residue and shall deal with it in the following manner:

(a) My Estate Trustee shall pay the net income to during 's lifetime.

(b) Until the death of :

(i) My Estate Trustee shall pay to or use for 's maintenance such amounts out of the capital of the Family Trust as my Estate Trustee in the exercise of an absolute discretion considers appropriate.

(ii) My Estate Trustee shall pay to one or more of my children and to the exclusion of any one or more of my children or to use for the maintenance and education of one or more of my children and to the exclusion of any one or more of my children, such amounts out of the capital of the Family Trust as my Estate Trustee in the exercise of an absolute discretion considers appropriate.

(c) Upon the death of , my Estate Trustee shall divide the Family Trust among my issue in equal shares *per stirpes*.

Commentary: There are many variations of the family trust, and their provisions are usually the result of canvassing the real interests of the testator.

These trusts do not qualify for a deferral of capital gains tax liabilities (see the annotation to precedent E-7).

E-10 FAILURE OF SPOUSE AND LINEAL DESCENDANTS.

Short description: This precedent creates an equal distribution among named beneficiaries in the event the spouse and all lineal descendants of the testator are deceased and the residue of the estate remains to be distributed.

FAILURE OF GIFTS

If none of my [husband], my children or my more remote issue live to acquire an absolutely vested interest in my estate, my Estate Trustee shall divide the residue of my estate or the amount then remaining, as the case may be, into the number of equal parts necessary to give effect to the following distribution:

Commentary: This is a typical clause in a will where the children of the testator are young. It anticipates the possibility that neither the spouse nor the children will live to inherit, as might happen if all are killed in an accident or if the children survive their parents but die, leaving no issue, before the age specified for final distribution. In such a case, this clause appoints the final alternative beneficiaries.

As a practical matter it is essential, if husband and wife are making "mirror" wills, that this alternative distribution be the same for both wills. Otherwise, the distribution is a family lottery, where, for example, if the husband survives his wife, then her estate will pass to him and to his estate, and his alternative beneficiaries will inherit, even though his survivorship may be as short as 31 days.

E-11 FAILURE OF SPOUSE AND ISSUE — DIVISION AMONG NAMED BENEFICIARIES.

Short description: This is a variation of precedent E-10. Where all of the spouse and lineal descendants of the testator have died before the estate has finally been disposed of, the estate is divided between named beneficiaries or the whole paid to the survivor of them.

FAILURE OF GIFTS

If as the result of the death of all of my [husband] and issue, some or all of the benefits provided in my Will have failed, then I direct that any then residue be divided equally between   and   and if one of them is not then living, the residue shall be paid to the survivor of them.

Commentary: See the discussion following precedent E-10, which is equally applicable to this precedent.

E-12 ANNUITY FOR NAMED BENEFICIARY.

Short description: The trustee is directed to set aside a fund to provide an annuity for a named beneficiary.

Annuity

My Estate Trustee shall pay to my [wife], , an annuity in the amount of $ a year in equal monthly instalments during 's lifetime. I authorize my Estate Trustee to set aside a fund at such time as my Estate Trustee considers advisable, and which in the exercise of an absolute discretion is an amount which my Estate Trustee considers will be sufficient to produce revenue to provide for such annuity for my [wife].

Until such fund is set aside, my Estate Trustee shall pay such annuity out of the residue of my estate, first out of income. When such fund has been set aside there shall be no further liability on the remainder of my estate for the payment of such annuity.

If in any year after such fund is set aside the net income is more than sufficient to provide for the annuity, the surplus income in that year shall be capitalized. After [twenty-one (21)] years from the date of my death, the surplus income shall be paid to .

If in any year the net income is insufficient to provide for the annuity, the deficiency in that year shall be made up out of the capital of the fund.

Upon the death of my [wife], the fund remaining, including any accumulations of income, shall [*specify*].

Commentary: It may be convenient for the trustee who is required to pay an annuity to a beneficiary to set aside a portion of the estate to satisfy that annuity. The income of the fund will be liable for the annuity. However, if that income is insufficient, the trustee may draw upon the capital. Note the final distribution of the fund, a provision you will want to be careful not to overlook.

An alternative to this financing arrangement for the annuity is to direct the trustee to purchase an annuity from a life insurance company if that is financially and practically more convenient.

E-13 RESIDUE IF SPOUSE SURVIVES — MULTIPLE TAX-PLANNED TRUSTS.

Short description: This precedent creates multiple trusts and provides for the division of the estate into parts to create:

(a) an outright distribution to a surviving spouse;
(b) an exclusive spouse trust (see precedent E-7); and
(c) a form of "family" trust which sprinkles income and capital among a spouse, a child and issue of that child (a variation of the "Family Trust" in precedent E-9).

RESIDUE IF [WIFE] SURVIVES

If my [wife], , is living on the thirtieth day following the date of my death, my Estate Trustee shall divide the residue of my estate into three parts. The amount of each part and the assets of my estate to be allocated to each part shall be determined by my Estate Trustee in the exercise of an absolute discretion, and his or her decision in this regard shall be binding on all persons interested in my estate.

A. [Wife's] Part

One of such parts shall be called "my [Wife's] Part" and such part shall be transferred to my [wife], , for [her] own use absolutely.

B. [Wife's] Trust

One of such parts shall be called "my [Wife's] Trust". My Estate Trustee shall set aside my [Wife's] Trust upon trust and during the lifetime of my [wife] shall pay the net income to my [wife] and such amounts out of the capital of my [Wife's] Trust as my Estate Trustee shall in the exercise of an absolute discretion consider appropriate for my [wife's] support and benefit.

C. [Wife and Daughter's] Trust

One of such parts shall be called "my [Wife and Daughter's] Trust" and my Estate Trustee shall set aside my [Wife and Daughter's] Trust upon trust. During the lifetime of my [wife], :

(a) My Estate Trustee shall pay such amounts of the net income and out of the capital of my [Wife and Daughter's] Trust to or for such one or more of my [wife] and my [daughter], , and any issue of my [daughter], and to the exclusion of any one or more of them, all as my Estate Trustee in the exercise of an absolute discretion considers appropriate. Any income not so paid in any year shall be accumulated and added to the capital of my [Wife and Daughter's] Trust.

(b) After the [twenty-first] anniversary of the date of my death, the whole of the net income shall be paid to or for such one or more of my [wife] and my [daughter], any issue of my [daughter], and to the exclusion of any one or more of them, all as my Estate Trustee in the exercise of an absolute discretion considers appropriate.

Residue — Children's Provisions

Upon the death of the survivor of my [wife] and me, my Estate Trustee shall divide the residue of my estate (being my [Wife and Daughter's] Trust and my [Wife's] Trust, or the whole residue, as the case may be) into a number of equal parts so that there is:

(a) one such part for each child of mine living at the death of the survivor of my [wife] and me, and

(b) one such part for each child of mine not then living with issue then living.

My Estate Trustee shall deal with such parts as follows: [*specify*].

Commentary: This precedent is created exclusively for tax purposes so that advantage may be taken of capital gains deferrals where necessary and appropriate. If the plan is to create tax results, then the spouse and possibly the children should be very much part of the planning process to ensure that they understand the purpose of the multiple trust will.

It is recommended that the junior drafter not use this clause without advice from estate and tax specialists.

F. PAYMENTS FOR MINORS, POWERS OF TRUSTEE, GENERAL CLAUSES, TESTIMONIUM

The clauses in this section are varied. They are the clauses usually referred to as "boilerplate", which tends to derogate from the significance of including them. Taken together, they complete the structure of the will, including execution.

The "Powers of Trustee" clauses (see precedent F-2) govern the behaviour of the trustee, and, when properly used, will create a flexible and manageable administration and tax efficiency. Each clause has a commentary which should be fully understood before the clause is incorporated into a will.

Precedent F-8 deals with compensation for the trustee. The topic of compensation for executors and trustees is more widely discussed in section G.

Proper execution of the will, as demonstrated in the testimonium (see precedent F-9), is further discussed in Chapter 7.

F-1 PAYMENTS FOR MINORS.

Short description: This clause permits the trustee to pay out money on behalf of children whose shares are being held in trust.

PAYMENTS FOR MINORS

If any person becomes entitled to receive any share of my estate while under the age of majority, I direct my Estate Trustee to keep that share invested until such person attains the age of majority. In the meantime, my Estate Trustee shall pay or apply such amounts out of the income and capital as my Estate Trustee in the exercise of an absolute discretion considers advisable for the benefit of such person.

I authorize my Estate Trustee to make any payments for any person under the age of majority which my Estate Trustee is entitled to make under the terms of my Will to a parent or guardian or other person standing *in loco parentis* to such person, or to make any such payment directly to such person or to any other person for such person, all as my Estate Trustee in the exercise of an absolute discretion considers appropriate. Any evidence that my Estate Trustee has made any payment shall be a sufficient discharge to my Estate Trustee.

Commentary: This clause is almost always included in wills. Parents and other persons standing *in loco parentis* are not guardians of the children's property unless so appointed by the court. Thus, there is no one to whom a trustee could make a distribution who at law can give the trustee a proper receipt, and so the trustee is not discharged by making the payment. Obviously, the trustee needs authority to make payments out of the trust funds held for children and be confident that this will not create liability. Hence this clause.

See the *Children's Law Reform Act*, ss. 47 to 60.[7]

F-2 POWERS OF TRUSTEE.

Short description: The *Trustee Act* provides for the compensation of the trustee and enumerates powers and authorities that a trustee is granted. In order to empower the trustee to manage an estate in a manner different from that specified in the *Trustee Act*, a clause such as the one given here needs to be included in the will.

This precedent contains a standard set of powers for wills of average complexity. For other or more complex situations, refer to precedents H-1 to H-4.

[7] Section 58 amended 1993, c. 27, Sch.

The following is one precedent. Owing to its length, commentary is provided throughout rather than at the end.

POWERS OF ESTATE TRUSTEE

In order to carry out the trusts of my Will, I give my Estate Trustee the following powers to be used in the exercise of an absolute discretion at any time:

INVESTMENTS

My Estate Trustee shall make any investments for my estate that my Estate Trustee considers appropriate [including units or other interests of any mutual funds, common trust funds, unit trusts or similar investments],without being limited to those investments authorized by law for trustees. My Estate Trustee shall not be liable for any loss that may happen to my estate as a result of any investment made by my Estate Trustee in good faith.

. . . . .

Commentary: Sections 26 and 27 of the *Trustee Act* create classes of investments in which trustees may invest. These include government and municipal securities, mortgages and real estate, loan corporation debentures, trust company guaranteed investments, secured bonds, corporate securities, preferred shares, etc.

The *Trustee Act* is legislation which has been inherited from England and amended many times over the centuries to create classes of investments for trustees. Since these provisions do not reflect current economic times, there is need in the will for a clause designed to take the trustee out of that legislation and ensure that he or she has a broader scope and may invest in anything considered appropriate. Of course, the trustee must still exercise prudence and show good faith in the management of the trust assets. Failure to do so would be a breach of trust in most circumstances.

Having taken the trustee outside ss. 26 and 27 of the *Trustee Act*, it is essential that you be able to describe this investment clause to testators since the powers appear sweeping. As a practical matter, I discuss with testators whether it is appropriate to give a broad, flexible hand to the trustee in managing the assets of the estate, particularly where there are ongoing trusts created by the will. Where testators express some reservation about giving such broad powers to their trustees, I suggest that the problem may lie in the choice of trustee rather than in the investment clause.

Note the reference in square brackets to mutual funds and similar investments. Just after the first edition of this book was released, *Haslam* v. *Haslam* (1994), 114 D.L.R. (4th) 562, 3 E.T.R. (2d) 206 (Ont. Ct. (Gen. Div.)), was reported. Rosenberg J. held that mutual funds were not authorized investments permitted by ss. 26 and 27 of the *Trustee Act*. In *obiter*, he said that even the *usual* (emphasis mine) investment clause in most wills and trusts would not be wide enough to permit investment in mutual funds.

If you add the bracketed words to the investment clause, that clause should be wide enough to permit investment in mutual funds. However, you might also want to include clauses which address more specifically the problems identified by Rosenberg J. For example, Rosenberg J. said that one problem with mutual funds is that trustees improperly delegate their obligation to make investment decisions to the mutual fund managers. To address this problem, you could add these words to your clause:

> It is my wish that my Estate Trustees consider the advice of   . They may rely on the advice of and delegate to such investment counsel, broker or agent the management of part or all of my estate as they consider appropriate from time to time on a discretionary basis.

You will also have to consider, in the context of mutual and other funds, whether trust companies should be permitted to invest in their own common and pooled funds. If so, the following should be added:

> I specifically authorize my Estate Trustee to invest in any mutual funds or pooled investments, including one or more of the common trust funds administered by Trust Corporation for the collective investment of moneys belonging to estates and trusts in its care.

I refer you to a superb paper given at the 1996 Law Society of Upper Canada Special Lectures by Madam Justice Susan Greer entitled "Developments in the Law Governing Trustees' Investment Powers".

> . . . . .
>
> **SELLING AND DISPOSING**
>
> My Estate Trustee shall realize or dispose of the assets of my estate, subject to the trusts of my Will, in any manner and on any terms.
>
> **RETENTION OF ASSETS**
>
> My Estate Trustee shall hold any of my assets in the form in which they may be at the time of my death for any length of time, whether or not they might not be assets in which trustees would otherwise be entitled to invest trust moneys. Those assets so retained shall be deemed to be authorized investments.
>
> . . . . .

Commentary: The subparagraphs headed "Investments", "Selling and Disposing" and "Retention of Assets" ensure that the trustee does not have to sell original assets when that may not be appropriate, and may choose the ongoing investments in order to reflect both an even hand between the beneficiaries and current economic conditions.

. . . . .

Distribution in Specie

My Estate Trustee shall make any division, distribution or allocation of the assets of my estate in kind and at such valuations as my Estate Trustee in the exercise of an absolute discretion considers appropriate. In determining such valuations, my Estate Trustee may consider such future expectations for such assets as my Estate Trustee in the exercise of an absolute discretion considers appropriate, including any tax liability or credit. Any decision of my Estate Trustee in this regard shall be binding on all persons concerned.

. . . . .

Commentary: This subparagraph ensures that the trustee does not have to sell assets in order to make a distribution. The trustee may distribute assets in kind, and the only real issue is valuation of those assets. The subparagraph directs the trustee to exercise discretion in fixing values on different kinds of assets.

. . . . .

Employment of Agents

If my Estate Trustee considers it necessary to engage any corporation or person to carry out some or all of the directions in my Will, my Estate Trustee may employ such corporation or person and may pay compensation out of my estate, all as my Estate Trustee considers appropriate.

. . . . .

Commentary: The trustee may hire agents including lawyers, accountants, real estate agents, etc., and may compensate those agents out of the trust fund. The agents' fees may be deducted from the trustee's compensation.

. . . . .

REAL PROPERTY

If any real or leasehold property forms part of my estate, my Estate Trustee may lease such property for any term and subject to such conditions as my Estate Trustee considers appropriate. My Estate Trustee may accept surrenders of leases and tenancies, may pay money out of the income or capital of my estate for repairs and improvements and may generally manage the property. My Estate Trustee may give any options that my Estate Trustee may consider advisable. My Estate Trustee may renew any mortgage, may borrow money on any real estate upon any mortgage and may pay off any mortgage which may exist at my death or at any renewal.

. . . . .

Commentary: This subparagraph is important if real estate is to be held in the trust fund. Sections 26 and 27 of the *Trustee Act*, which set out the investments that are authorized for trustees, do not include real estate as an authorized investment. Also, whereas first mortgages are permitted under those sections, the common law restricts the amount of those mortgages to 75% of the value of the real property. Hence this subparagraph, which is intended to assist the trustee who does not wish to sell real estate if the timing is inappropriate and who wishes to manage the real estate in a business-like manner.

. . . . .

Loans to Beneficiaries

My Estate Trustee may lend money or other assets of my estate to any beneficiary, or guarantee any loans for any beneficiary or for any company owned or controlled by my estate or by a beneficiary, or in which my estate or a beneficiary may have an interest, upon such terms, with or without interest, and with or without security, all as my Estate Trustee in the exercise of an absolute discretion considers appropriate.

. . . . .

Commentary: Loans to beneficiaries is a useful subparagraph. I see it as an adjunct to the discretion to encroach out of the trust fund for beneficiaries. For example, a beneficiary who would like a capital encroachment to purchase a house might well be told that the estate will not make the encroachment but will take back a mortgage for part of the purchase price. This protects the asset for the estate and prevents the beneficiary from exhausting the trust fund.

. . . . .

Borrowing

My Estate Trustee may borrow on behalf of my estate such amounts as my Estate Trustee considers appropriate, and may mortgage or otherwise charge any of the assets of my estate.

. . . . .

Commentary: Trustees are not entitled to borrow without specific authority to do so. Generally, trustees would not want to borrow; however, it may be necessary to bridge finance where liquid assets are not available to pay debts.

. . . . .

<u>SETTLEMENT OF CLAIMS</u>

Without the consent of any person interested under my Will, my Estate Trustee may compromise, settle or waive any claim at any time due to or by my estate and may make any agreement with any person, government or corporation which shall be binding upon all persons interested in my estate.

. . . . .

Commentary: Generally, trustees should not settle claims against the estate without the benefit of a court order and full litigation. However, that is not always practical, and so trustees should be given power to unilaterally settle claims. These may be claims by a surviving spouse, by the beneficiaries, or indeed by Revenue Canada.

. . . . .

<u>SECURITIES</u>

My Estate Trustee may deal with any securities, shares or other interests of any corporation which is held by my estate, to the same extent as if I were alive. My Estate Trustee may take up new or further shares or other interests, may join in any reorganization, may exchange shares or other interests, and may give or accept and exercise options. My Estate Trustee may pay out of my estate any moneys which may be necessary for any of these purposes.

. . . . .

Commentary: This subparagraph is directed to the continued holding of shares of private corporations, which would likely not be an authorized investment under the *Trustee Act*.

. . . . .

Transactions with Estate Trustee

In my Estate Trustee's personal capacity, my Estate Trustee may purchase assets from my estate [if the purchase price and other terms are unanimously approved by my Estate Trustee and by the adult beneficiaries of my estate]. My Estate Trustee shall not be required to obtain the approval of any Court for such purchase.

Commentary: At common law, a trustee is not entitled to self-deal. However, it may be that a trustee would want to purchase an asset such as a piece of real estate from the estate. Generally, the court would have to authorize such a transaction unless a clause similar to this subparagraph is included in the will.

F-3 RRSP CONTRIBUTIONS.

Short description: The testator directs the trustee to make a last contribution to his or her RRSP after the date of death.

RRSP CONTRIBUTIONS

My Estate Trustee shall make such contribution as my Estate Trustee in the exercise of an absolute discretion considers appropriate to any registered retirement savings plan of which I am the annuitant at the date of my death at any time between the date of my death and sixty days after the end of the calendar year in which I die.

Commentary: Section 146[8] of the *Income Tax Act* (Canada) provides that the executor and trustee of a deceased person is entitled to make a contribution to the RRSP of the deceased at any time after the date of death up to 60 days after the calendar year end. The sole purpose is to ensure that the contribution is made and the tax deduction taken in the terminal return (filed for the period January 1st to the date of death). Where there is a surviving spouse to whom the RRSP can be rolled over, this can be an attractive deduction for the terminal return. It is a good idea to include this precedent in the will so that no one forgets to take advantage of the contribution provisions where there is a surviving spouse.

F-4 EXCLUSION OF ILLEGITIMATES.

Short description: This clause is useful where the testator does not want children born outside of marriage to inherit.

DEFINITION OF RELATIONSHIPS

Any reference in my Will to a person in terms of a relationship to another person determined by blood or marriage shall not include a person born outside marriage or a person who comes within the description traced through another person who was born outside marriage. Any person who has been legally adopted shall be regarded as having been born in the marriage of his or her adopting parent.

Commentary: This paragraph must be drawn to the attention of the testator. Until 1978, illegitimate children were not included in class

[8] Amended 1994, c. 7, Sch. II, s. 117; *idem*, Sch. VII, s. 13; *idem*, Sch. VIII, s. 82; 1994, c. 21, ss. 69, 136; 1995, c. 3, s. 43.

descriptions of beneficiaries such as children, issue, lineal descendants, etc. Then in 1978, Ontario's law was changed dramatically by the *Children's Law Reform Act*, which abolished the status of illegitimacy (see s. 1(4) of the current Act). As a practical matter, then, if testators wish to exclude illegitimates, this must be done by the will; otherwise, illegitimates are automatically included. You might add to this clause the following:

> If a child of mine has a child born outside of marriage, and my child acknowledges in writing to my Estate Trustees that such child shall be considered his or her child for all purposes of my Will, my Estate Trustees shall not exclude such child born outside of marriage or a person who comes within the description traced through that child.

F-5 EXCLUSIONS FROM NET FAMILY PROPERTY.

Short description: Here the testator excludes the property inherited by his or her beneficiaries from division under the *Family Law Act*.

> **EXCLUSIONS FROM NET FAMILY PROPERTY**
>
> I declare that the income, including capital gains, arising from any interest passing to a beneficiary under my Will shall be excluded from such beneficiary's net family property or from the value of the beneficiary's assets on the death, divorce or separation of such beneficiary, pursuant to the *Family Law Act*, R.S.O. 1990, c. F.3.

All gifts made to a beneficiary shall be the separate property of my beneficiaries and shall not fall into any Community of Property or be subject to any other matrimonial rights of the spouses of my beneficiaries and shall not be liable for the obligations of any such spouses or Community. All such gifts shall not be subject to seizure for the payment of any debts of beneficiaries or their representatives while in the possession and control of my Estate Trustee.

Commentary: Section 4 of the *Family Law Act* is the definition section and s. 4(2) contains a definition of excluded property. This section provides for the exclusion of property acquired by gift or inheritance *after the date of the marriage* and of income from that gifted or inherited property if the donor or testator has expressly stated that it is to be excluded. Note that it is only property inherited during the term of the marriage which enjoys this exclusion. Property which is brought into the marriage and which was inherited or gifted *prior* to the date of the marriage is treated like other assets brought into the marriage.

It is particularly important that you draw this precedent to the attention of the testator. It is my standard practice to include this provision to confirm that inheritances received by a beneficiary do not form part of that beneficiary's net family property under the *Family Law Act* and to declare that income earned by the inheritance is also excluded. Inherited property is excluded automatically from the beneficiary's net family property in the situation discussed in the previous paragraph; however, the income is only excluded if the testator specifically says so in the will. I usually remind testators that this provision is not intended to defeat spouses, but to give a beneficiary a choice where he or she might be having marital difficulties, since inherited property is clearly not property created by the spouses' partnership.

F-6 SELECTION OF PROPERTY IN SATISFACTION OF SPOUSAL CLAIM.

Short description: If the surviving spouse successfully sues for equalization under the *Family Law Act*, the trustee chooses the property to satisfy the claim.

> **SELECTION OF PROPERTY IN SATISFACTION OF CLAIM**
>
> If my [wife] becomes entitled to receive an interest in my net family property as defined in the *Family Law Act*, R.S.O. 1990, c. F.3, or its successor Act, my Estate Trustee shall in the exercise of an absolute discretion determine which of my properties shall be transferred and delivered to my [wife] or sold for the purpose of satisfying any Judgment, Order or Settlement in favour of my [wife] under the *Family Law Act* or its successor Act.

Commentary: This clause simply gives the trustee authority to allocate specific assets to satisfy the claim of a spouse who is successful under s. 6 of the *Family Law Act*. Obviously, if the court order directs specific property as the source of the settlement, then this paragraph is ineffective.

F-7 SUITS BY BENEFICIARIES.

Short description: Under this clause, a beneficiary who sues will be disinherited.

SUITS BY BENEFICIARIES

If any beneficiary commences any litigation in connection with any of the provisions of my Will other than for any necessary judicial interpretation thereof or for the assistance of the Court in the course of administration, all benefits to which such person would have been entitled shall immediately cease. I direct that such benefits so revoked shall become part of the residue of my estate to be distributed as if such person had predeceased me and had left no issue surviving me.

Commentary: This clause cannot prevent litigation, and so it is ineffective in that sense. However, these types of draconian, *in terrorem* clauses can serve a practical purpose in a will by frightening beneficiaries who are tempted to involve the estate in frivolous litigation.

F-8 COMPENSATION FOR TRUSTEE.

Short description: The trustee may be paid for work in progress without the necessity of court approval.

COMPENSATION

I authorize my Estate Trustee to take and transfer at reasonable intervals from the income and/or capital of my estate amounts on account of his or her compensation which my Estate Trustee reasonably anticipates will be requested at the end of the accounting period in progress, either upon the audit of the estate accounts or on approval by the beneficiaries of my estate. If the amount subsequently awarded on Court audit or agreed to by the beneficiaries is less than the amount so taken, the excess shall be repaid to my estate without interest.

Commentary: See precedent G-1 for commentary on this clause. Precedents G-2 to G-4 contain variations of the compensation clause.

F-9 TESTIMONIUM.

Short description: The testator and the witnesses sign together, with all the statutory formalities.

IN TESTIMONY WHEREOF I have to my Will, which is written upon this and preceding pages of paper, subscribed my name the day and year first above written.

SIGNED by , as	)	
[his] Will, in the presence	)	
of us both, present at the	)	
same time, who at [his]	)	____________
request, in [his] presence	)	[*Signature of testator*]
and in the presence of	)	
each other have subscribed	)	
our names as witnesses:	)	
	)	
	)	

1. ______________________)
Signature of witness)
)
______________________)
Print name)
)
______________________)
Address)
)
______________________)
Occupation)
)
)
2. ______________________)
Signature of witness)
)
______________________)
Print name)
)
______________________)
Address)
)
______________________)
Occupation)

Commentary: The testimonium is relatively straightforward. Proper execution of a will is extremely important since failure to meet the requirements of Ontario law for proper execution may invalidate the will. Sections 4 to 7 of the *Succession Law Reform Act* provide for the formalities of execution. See precedents M-2 and M-3 and the general comments at the beginning of Chapter 7 for a broader discussion.

G. COMPENSATION FOR EXECUTORS AND TRUSTEES

All executors, trustees and administrators are entitled to be compensated for their work in the administration of estates of deceased persons. This is in virtue of s. 61 of the *Trustee Act*:

> 61(1) A trustee, guardian or personal representative is entitled to such fair and reasonable allowance for the care, pains and trouble, and the time expended in and about the estate, as may be allowed by a judge of the Ontario Court (General Division).
>
> (2) The amount of such compensation may be settled although the estate is not before the court in an action.
>
> (3) The judge, in passing the accounts of a trustee or of a personal representative or guardian, may from time to time allow a fair and reasonable allowance for care, pains and trouble, and time expended in or about the estate.
>
> (4) Where a barrister or solicitor is a trustee, guardian or personal representative, and has rendered necessary professional services to the estate, regard may be had in making the allowance to such circumstance, and the allowance shall be increased by such amount as may be considered fair and reasonable in respect of such services.
>
> (5) Nothing in this section applies where the allowance is fixed by the instrument creating the trust.

You will note at once that the statute is silent as to the amount that is appropriate. In Ontario, as in other Canadian jurisdictions, there is no tariff which can be applied to the estate to determine an amount of compensation. However, over the years, the courts have applied a "rule of thumb" tariff, and it is departed from only in special circumstances. In such cases, the court will reduce or increase the compensation or will permit a special fee (usually supported by a memorandum).

The "tariff" at its present levels is as follows:

(a) 2½% of capital receipts;
(b) 2½% of capital disbursements;
(c) 2½% of income receipts;
(d) 2½% of income disbursements; and
(e) for ongoing trusts, 2/5 of 1% of the average annual market value of the trust assets as a fee for ongoing care and management.

While attempts to increase the percentages have been refused by the courts in recent cases, it is possible to have the testator in the will, or the beneficiaries after the date of death, agree to higher percentages which are felt to more properly reflect the nature of the work involved in the administration of the estate.

You are referred to F.D. Baker, *Widdifield on Executors' Accounts*, 5th ed. (Toronto, Carswell, 1967) [a new edition will be published in 1997], and Brian A. Schnurr, "Quantifying Executors' Compensation: Law and Procedure" (1992), 11 E. & T.J. 134.

G-1 COMPENSATION WITHOUT PASSING ACCOUNTS.

Short description: This precedent authorizes the trustee to be paid for work in progress without the necessity of court approval.

COMPENSATION

I authorize my Estate Trustee to take and transfer at reasonable intervals from the income and capital of my estate amounts on account of compensation which my Estate Trustee reasonably anticipates will be requested at the end of the accounting period in progress, either upon the audit of the estate accounts or on approval by the beneficiaries of my estate. If the amount subsequently awarded on Court audit or agreed to by the beneficiaries is less than the amount so taken, the excess shall be repaid to my estate without interest.

Commentary: The decision in *Knoch (Re)* (1982), 12 E.T.R. 162 (Ont. Surr. Ct.), finally put an end to the practice of trustees' taking their compensation in advance of the court determining and ordering that compensation. Until then, it had been the usual practice of trustees to "pre-take" their compensation and have it reviewed by the court at a later date.

However, it is the view of most practitioners and trust companies that trustees do not overpay themselves by taking instalments of compensation. Further, since compensation is taxable in the hands of the trustee, it is better that the compensation be paid on a regular basis to avoid an uneven tax burden on the trustee. Finally, a more even cash flow in the estate is created by having the compensation paid regularly rather than by having it all taken in, say, the fifth year on a court audit. For all these reasons, pre-taking is considered to be appropriate, and so, in cases where trustees will want to be paid, I always include this precedent in the will. It would be a pity to have those trustees passing their accounts in court on a regular basis when the only purpose is to fix compensation.

G-2 EXECUTOR'S COMPENSATION — MEMORANDUM SETTING OUT AMOUNT.

Short description: A memorandum setting out the compensation for the executor and trustee is incorporated into the will.

FEES

I direct that shall be entitled to receive, and shall be paid out of my estate, as compensation for acting as the Executor and Trustee (or one of the Executors and Trustees) of my Will, the fees and other compensation provided for in the memorandum annexed to my Will, dated the day of , 19 , and signed by me, prior to the execution of my Will. I declare that the memorandum is incorporated in my Will.

Commentary: Section 61(5) of the *Trustee Act* provides that the testator may direct by will the fee to be paid to the trustee. Such a memorandum of compensation is often preferred by trust companies in order to ensure that there is no disagreement after the date of death about the amount of compensation to which the trustee is entitled. However, the use of such a memorandum is not restricted to trust companies, and the testator and any trustee may decide among themselves as to the fee to be paid.

G-3 EXECUTOR'S COMPENSATION — WILL INCORPORATES MEMORANDUM SETTING OUT AMOUNT.

Short description: A memorandum of compensation is included in the will and pre-taking of that compensation is authorized.

EXECUTOR'S COMPENSATION

I declare and direct that   shall be entitled to receive, and shall be paid out of my estate, as compensation for acting as Executor and Trustee of my Will, the fees and other compensation provided for in the memorandum annexed to my Will, dated the   day of   , 19 , and signed by me, prior to the execution of my Will, and which is incorporated in my Will.

I authorize my Estate Trustee to take and transfer at reasonable intervals from the income and capital of my estate amounts on account of compensation which my Estate Trustee reasonably anticipates will be requested at the end of the accounting period in progress, either upon the audit of the estate accounts or on approval by the beneficiaries of my estate. If the amount subsequently awarded on Court audit or agreed to by the beneficiaries is less than the amount so taken, the excess shall be repaid to my estate without interest.

Commentary: This precedent is simply a variation of precedents G-1 and G-2, ensuring that not only are the trustees paid according to a memorandum, but they may pre-take their compensation. The pre-taking clause is probably not necessary where the compensation is authorized by a memorandum; however, you should check the text of the memorandum to be sure.

G-4 FEES FOR CONTINGENT EXECUTOR.

Short description: A memorandum of compensation is provided for a contingent executor. Pre-taking of compensation is authorized for all executors.

FEES FOR CONTINGENT EXECUTOR

I direct that if   becomes the Executor and Trustee (or one of the Executors and Trustees) of my Will,   shall be entitled to receive, and shall be paid out of my estate, as compensation for acting as the Executor and Trustee (or one of the Executors and Trustees) of my Will, the fees and other compensation provided for in the memorandum annexed to my Will, dated the   day of   , 19   , and signed by me, prior to the execution of my Will, and which is incorporated in my Will.

I authorize my Estate Trustee to take and transfer at reasonable intervals from the income and capital of my estate amounts on account of compensation which my Estate Trustee reasonably anticipates will be requested at the end of the accounting period in progress, either upon the audit of the estate accounts or on approval by the beneficiaries of my estate. If the amount subsequently awarded on Court audit or agreed to by the beneficiaries is less than the amount so taken, the excess shall be repaid to my estate without interest.

Commentary: This would be a typical paragraph where a trust company is to act on the administration in the event that the surviving spouse or other named trustee cannot or will not act. Should that be the case, then the trust company may prefer to have the memorandum of compensation included in the will.

See precedent G-1 with respect to pre-taking compensation.

A sample compensation agreement, which has been provided by the Canada Trust Company, follows.

Canada Trust

COMPENSATION AGREEMENT

I agree that the compensation which shall be paid to The Canada Trust Company ("Canada Trust") for its services performed in the capacity of executor and trustee of my estate and any trusts established under my Will shall be as follows:

Estate Administration
Payable on the basis of the value of capital assets realized at the following rates:

5% on the first $250,000
4% on the next $750,000
3% on the balance

(minimum fee $2,500)

This one-time fee is payable in interim amounts related to the work done and time spent on my estate during the first year. At the end of the first year, any assets not then realized will be deemed to be realized at fair market value.

Assets in a Summit/FCA or other Canada Trust account held at the time of death, which pass on to my estate will receive a reduction of 25% on the rates indicated above.

Asset Management
Payable on the average market value of assets under administration at the following rates:

0.6% per annum on the first $250,000
0.5% per annum on the next $250,000
0.4% per annum on the balance

(minimum annual fee $600)

Compensation shall be charged from the end of the first year of the estate or, in the case of any trusts established under my Will, from the date of inception of the trusts. Fees are payable monthly or at such other intervals as Canada Trust may determine.

Income Collection
Payable on income as collected at a rate of 6%.

Tax Services
Payable in accordance with Canada Trust's scale of fees in effect from time to time.

Special Services
Should it be necessary for Canada Trust to render services for the administration of the estate or trusts which are beyond the scope of those usually provided, Canada Trust shall be entitled to additional compensation on such basis as may be approved by the beneficiaries or which the Court may determine to be fair and reasonable.

Real Estate Commission
Real estate commission paid for the sale or leasing of real property held in the estate or trusts shall be an additional disbursement of the estate or trust, whether paid to the Real Estate Division of Canada Trust or to any other broker, provided that it does not exceed the rate of commission prevailing in the area where the real estate is located.

> Canada Trust will rebate to my estate 25% of the listing portion of the commission paid to its Real Estate Division on the sale of real property of my estate.

Reimbursement of Expenses
Canada Trust is to be reimbursed for expenses other than normal out-of-pocket expenses incurred in the administration of the estate or trusts established under my Will.

Rate Changes
The rates indicated for Asset Management and Income Collection may be changed by Canada Trust following five years after the date of my death to its scale of fees in effect from time to time.

Co-Trustee's Compensation
The compensation of co-executors or co-trustees, if any, will be in addition to the fees payable to Canada Trust as provided above.

Termination
This agreement may be terminated during my lifetime by either me or Canada Trust and such termination will be effective upon the receipt of written notice by the other party.

____________________ Date	____________________ Testator/Testatrix
	____________________ The Canada Trust Company

H. MISCELLANEOUS ADDITIONAL CLAUSES

The precedents in this section may be added to the will following the "Powers of Trustee" precedents. They are useful in limited circumstances such as when the testator owns a business or corporation and wants the trustees to carry on the business for the benefit of the estate.

H-1 PERPETUITY CLAUSE.

Short description: This clause directs an absolute vesting of interest immediately before a perpetuity date.

PERPETUITY CLAUSE

Notwithstanding anything in my Will, any interest in my estate directed to be held for the benefit of any person shall vest absolutely in the person for whom such interest is held and who, immediately before such vesting, is entitled to receive the income of such interest, on the earlier of the following two dates:

(a) the date upon which such person is entitled absolutely to such interest, or

(b) the last day of the period of [twenty-one] years from the death of the last to survive me, my [husband] and my issue alive at my death.

Commentary: This is an unusual clause to include in a will unless trusts are directed to be held over long periods of time. There are common law and statutory rules preventing property from being held in trust beyond a perpetuity date. The purpose of these rules (which do not apply to charitable trusts) is to prevent the indefinite holding of property in trust. Most Canadian jurisdictions have perpetuities legislation. In Ontario it is the *Perpetuities Act*, R.S.O. 1990, c. P.9. The purpose of the precedent is to fix a vesting of interest at the time of distribution, just before the perpetuity period runs out.

H-2 COST OF LIVING INCREASE.

Short description: Specific payments are directed to be increased according to the cost of living index or according to a comparable index if the cost of living index is not published.

COST OF LIVING INCREASE

The amount of the payments required to be made pursuant to paragraph shall be increased in direct proportion to the increase in the Cost of Living Index published by Statistics Canada or the equivalent official statistical publication of the Government of Canada. For the purpose of this paragraph and paragraph , the Cost of Living Index at , in 19 , was and was based on the consumer prices for the year 19 equalling 100.

Commentary: Often testators will want to give a specific dollar amount (per month or other period) to a named beneficiary. This can be risky business in view of the fact that the purchasing power of money declines with increases in the cost of living. I try to discourage testators from setting specific dollar amounts, but if they are determined to do so, then I try to insist on including a provision for indexing. In order to draft this paragraph, you will have to call Statistics Canada for the pertinent information for your location.

H-3 CARRYING ON BUSINESS.

Short description: This clause directs the continuation of businesses of the deceased. It ensures continuity where a business is not to be wound up.

CARRYING ON BUSINESS

My Estate Trustee shall carry on any business, incorporated or otherwise, which I may own or in which I have an interest at the date of my death, for such length of time as my Estate Trustee considers to be in the best interests of my estate. My Estate Trustee shall do all things necessary or advisable for the carrying on, incorporation, winding up, amalgamation or disposal of any business or interest to the same extent as I could do if still living. My Estate Trustee shall not be responsible for any loss to my estate as a result of exercising these powers.

Commentary: Often beneficiaries will want to continue a business operated by the testator. This can be a burden on the trustees who may have no particular expertise in managing the business. Partly, the solution is a matter of ensuring an appropriate trustee, but also, the trustee should be allowed to hire agents and managers and do anything that seems appropriate for the particular business. The trustee should also be absolved from responsibility if things go wrong.

H-4 INDEBTEDNESS.

Short description: The trustee is directed to continue with promissory notes or guarantees of the indebtedness of third parties.

INDEBTEDNESS

If I am liable as maker of any promissory notes or as endorser or guarantor for any liability of any company or person, my Estate Trustee may renew the notes and guarantees or contracts evidencing such liability. For that purpose my Estate Trustee may enter into new notes or guarantees or contracts on behalf of my estate. It is my intention in conferring upon my Estate Trustee these powers and discretions to give my Estate Trustee those powers to assist in the gradual liquidation of the liabilities which I may be under in order that my estate or the companies or persons for whom I may be liable may not be unduly embarrassed.

Commentary: It may be appropriate for the trustee to gradually liquidate outstanding liabilities rather than pay them off immediately.

H-5 GOVERNING LAW.

Short description: The testator directs that the will be interpreted by Ontario law.

GOVERNING LAW

My Will shall be governed by and construed in accordance with the laws of the Province of Ontario.

Commentary: Non-common law jurisdictions may not recognize trusts in the sense that the laws in those jurisdictions do not recognize that legal ownership can be divided from beneficial ownership. This can give rise to interpretation problems. Therefore, it is useful to bring the will into Ontario or other provincial law, including its conflict of law provisions which stem from the common law and from ss. 34 to 41 of the *Succession Law Reform Act.*

H-6 HEADINGS.

Short description: As a matter of construction, headings do not affect the meaning of the paragraphs following.

HEADINGS

The paragraph headings used in my Will are for convenience only and shall not be construed to affect the meaning of a paragraph so headed.

Commentary: I do not usually include this clause in the will since headings, as a matter of construction, do not affect the paragraphs so headed. However, lay people who are reading the will may be misled by the headings, and so this paragraph can be useful as a practical matter.

I. FUNERAL, BURIAL AND DONATION OF BODY

The most obvious problem with including funeral instructions in wills is that the will is often not read until after the funeral and burial. I always advise my clients to ensure that other family members are made aware of such wishes prior to the testator's death. I also discourage elaborate instructions for funeral and burial unless the client wants to set out these instructions in a letter, a copy of which would be left with the will.

See the *Human Tissue Gift Act*, R.S.O. 1990, c. H.20.

I-1 CREMATION.

Short description: This paragraph directs that the testator wishes to be cremated.

CREMATION

It is my wish that I be cremated.

Commentary: I understand that some funeral homes, to avoid the possibility of contest from the next of kin, are reluctant to cremate a deceased person unless he or she has left instructions for that cremation. However, custody of the body belongs to the executor and trustee, and he or she is the one with authority to make the necessary funeral arrangements.

See A.H. Oosterhoff, "Disposition of Parts of the Body", *Wills and Succession*, 3rd ed. (Toronto, Carswell, 1990), p. 133.

I-2 FUNERAL.

Short description: The testator chooses his or her funeral home and directs burial in a specific plot.

> **FUNERAL**
>
> It is my wish that I be buried from [XYZ Funeral Home], in the [City] of , at [Hillview Cemetery], in plot number , in the most inexpensive casket possible with no services either at the funeral home or the grave.

Commentary: Funeral instructions in the will do not bind the trustee or the next of kin. They are an expression of the testator's wishes.

It is important to remind the testator that putting funeral instructions in the will may not ensure that his or her wishes in that regard are carried out since the will may not be looked at until long after the funeral has been completed.

I-3 FUNERAL INSTRUCTIONS.

Short description: The testator directs a closed casket, no viewing and only immediate family at the funeral.

FUNERAL INSTRUCTIONS

It is my wish that I be buried in a closed casket, that there be no viewing of my body and that only my immediate family attend the funeral.

Commentary: These instructions are completely within the discretion of the testator. He or she should be reminded, however, that relying solely on will instructions might be risky since the will is often not referred to until after the funeral and any mourning period is completed.

I-4 DONATION OF BODY.

Short description: The testator wishes his or her body to be donated to a particular medical school for research purposes.

DONATION OF BODY

I direct that my body be delivered to the Department of Anatomy of the University of (or to the nearest medical school) to be used for medical education and research.

Commentary: These kinds of clauses have no legal effect but are generally respected by the next of kin and the trustee. A variation would be donations of particular parts of the body such as eyes, lungs, kidneys, etc. Various charitable organizations such as the Kidney Foundation have sample clauses for such donations, and the testator may also sign his or her Ontario driver's licence to create the same results.

See Part II of the *Human Tissue Gift Act*, which provides for post-mortem gifts for transplant and other purposes.

Chapter 4

MULTIPLE AND INTERNATIONAL WILLS

It is not unusual for a testator to have assets in many jurisdictions. One will may be sufficient to dispose of those assets; however, there are two other possibilities.

The first is for the client to execute a separate will for the disposition of assets in each jurisdiction. Precedent J-1 demonstrates this sort of will. It refers to the "Canadian" assets but could as well refer to assets in another jurisdiction. The obvious pitfall is that you will have to ensure that each will suits the laws of the jurisdiction for which it is intended, and this is best achieved by having local counsel review it.

The second possibility for a client with assets in various jurisdictions is to have the client execute an international will. This kind of will is recognized by the *Succession Law Reform Act*, R.S.O. 1990, c. S.26. The main difficulty is not that this format is inappropriate, but rather that there are few relevant jurisdictions which are signatories to and have ratified the use of the Convention Providing a Uniform Law on the Form of an International Will.

Section 42 of the *Succession Law Reform Act* provides for the international will and contains the text of the convention. Sections 34 to 41 deal with conflict of laws, including the formal validity of wills and the rules for dispositions of personal and real property.

J-1 MULTIPLE WILLS.

Short description: A testator prepares separate wills for assets in several jurisdictions.

THIS IS THE WILL of me, , of the [City] of , in the [County] of , and Province of Ontario, made this day of , 19 , and by which I intend to dispose of my assets situate in the Dominion of Canada. I will refer to my Will as my "Canadian Will", to my assets situate in the Dominion of Canada as my "Canadian assets" and to my estate to be administered in the Dominion as my "Canadian estate".

I. REVOCATION

I revoke all Wills and Codicils previously made by me, pertaining to my Canadian assets.

II. EXECUTOR AND TRUSTEE

I appoint to be the Executor and Trustee of my Canadian Will. I will refer to the Executor and Trustee as my "Canadian Trustee".

III. GIFTS TO CANADIAN TRUSTEE

I give my Canadian assets to my Canadian Trustee upon the following trusts:

1. Debts and Death Taxes

My Canadian Trustee shall pay out of the capital of my Canadian estate all my just debts incurred in Canada (including any income taxes payable respecting my income in the year(s) prior to my death and in the year of my death to the date of my death), and testamentary expenses arising out of my Canadian estate, and all succession duties, estate, gift, inheritance and death taxes, imposed pursuant to the laws of Ontario or any other Canadian jurisdiction.

2. Conversion of my Assets

My Canadian Trustee shall call in my Canadian assets and shall sell such Canadian assets at such time, for such price and in such manner as my Canadian Trustee in the exercise of an absolute discretion considers appropriate. I authorize my Canadian Trustee to continue to hold any asset owned by me at the date of my death, without liability for loss or depreciation, for as long as my Canadian Trustee in the exercise of an absolute discretion considers appropriate, notwithstanding it may not be an investment in which a trustee may by law invest trust funds.

3. Residue

My Canadian Trustee shall hold and invest the residue of my Canadian estate upon the following trusts:

(a) My Canadian Trustee from time to time shall pay such amounts out of the net income derived from the residue of my Canadian estate and such amounts out of the capital thereof to or for my [daughter], , and my [son], , and to the exclusion of either of them for their support, education and advancement in life, all as [he *or* she] in the exercise of an absolute discretion considers appropriate.

(b) After [twenty-one] years from the date of my death, my Canadian Trustee shall divide the net income derived therefrom equally between my [son] and my [daughter], or shall pay the whole of the net income to the survivor of them.

(c) Upon [the first day of January, 2015], my Canadian Trustee shall divide the residue of my Canadian estate then remaining among my issue then living in equal shares *per stirpes*.

IV. PAYMENTS FOR MINORS

If any person should become entitled to receive any share of my Canadian estate while such person is under the age of majority, then I direct my Canadian Trustee to keep such share invested until such person attains the age of majority, and, in the meantime, to pay or apply the income and capital or so much thereof as my Canadian Trustee in the exercise of an absolute discretion considers necessary or advisable for the benefit of such person.

I authorize my Canadian Trustee to make any payments for any person under the age of majority which my Canadian Trustee is entitled to make under the terms of my Canadian Will to a parent or guardian or other person standing *in loco parentis* to such person, or to make any such payment directly to such person or to any other person for such person, all as my Canadian Trustee in the exercise of an absolute discretion considers appropriate. Any evidence that my Canadian Trustee has made any payment as an exercise of such discretion shall be a sufficient discharge to my Canadian Trustee without the requirement of any receipt.

V. POWERS OF CANADIAN TRUSTEE

In order to carry out the provisions of my Canadian Will, I give my Canadian Trustee the following powers to be used in the exercise of an absolute discretion at any time:

1. Investments

My Canadian Trustee may make any investments for my Canadian estate that my Canadian Trustee considers appropriate without being limited to those investments authorized by law for trustees, and my Canadian Trustee shall not be liable for any loss that may happen to my Canadian estate as a result of any investment made by my Canadian Trustee in good faith.

2. Selling and Disposing

My Canadian Trustee may sell, realize or otherwise dispose of all or any Canadian assets, investments or reinvestments, subject to the trusts hereof, at any time and in any manner, and either for money or for other Canadian assets or investments.

3. RETENTION OF ASSETS

My Canadian Trustee may hold any of my Canadian assets or investments in whole or in part in the form in which they may be at the time of my death for any length of time, notwithstanding that they may not be assets or investments in which trustees would otherwise be entitled by law to invest trust moneys, and those assets or investments so retained shall be deemed to be authorized investments for the purposes of my Canadian Will.

4. DISTRIBUTION IN SPECIE

My Canadian Trustee may make any division, distribution or allocation of the Canadian assets of my Canadian estate *in specie* and at such valuations as my Canadian Trustee in the exercise of an absolute discretion considers appropriate, and in determining such valuations, may consider such future expectations relating to such Canadian assets as my Canadian Trustee in the exercise of an absolute discretion considers appropriate, including any tax liability or credit. Any decision of my Canadian Trustee in this regard shall be binding on all persons concerned.

5. EMPLOYMENT OF AGENTS

If my Canadian Trustee, in carrying out any direction, considers it necessary in the exercise of an absolute discretion to engage a corporation, person or persons to carry out some or all of the directions, my Canadian Trustee may employ such corporation, person or persons and compensate such corporation, person or persons out of my Canadian estate, in such manner as my Canadian Trustee considers appropriate.

6. REAL PROPERTY

My Canadian Trustee may, at any time and for so long as any real or leasehold property forms part of my Canadian estate, let or lease such property from month to month, year to year or for any term of months and/or years and subject to such covenants and conditions as my Canadian Trustee considers appropriate. My Canadian Trustee may accept surrenders of leases and tenancies, expend money out of the income or capital of my Canadian estate for repairs and improvements and generally manage the property, and may give any options with respect to such property or properties as my Canadian Trustee considers advisable. My Canadian Trustee may renew and keep renewed any mortgage or mortgages upon real estate forming part of my Canadian estate, borrow money on any real estate forming part of my Canadian estate upon any mortgage or mortgages, and pay off any mortgage or mortgages which may be in existence at the time of my death or any renewal thereof.

7. LOANS TO BENEFICIARIES

My Canadian Trustee may lend money or other Canadian assets of my Canadian estate, or guarantee or continue any existing guarantees for loans, to any beneficiary of my Canadian Will or any company owned or controlled by my Canadian estate or by a beneficiary, or in which my Canadian estate or a beneficiary may have an interest, for such length of time and upon such terms and at such rate of interest or without interest and with such security or without security, all as my Canadian Trustee in the exercise of an absolute discretion considers appropriate.

8. BORROWING

My Canadian Trustee may borrow on behalf of my Canadian estate such amounts as my Canadian Trustee considers appropriate and mortgage, pledge, hypothecate or otherwise charge any of the Canadian assets of my Canadian estate.

9. SETTLEMENT OF CLAIMS

My Canadian Trustee may, without the consent of any persons interested under my Canadian Will and any Codicil, compromise, settle or waive any claim or claims at any time due to or by my Canadian estate and make any agreement with any other person, persons, government or corporation which shall be binding upon all persons interested under my Canadian Will and any Codicil.

10. SECURITIES

My Canadian Trustee may deal with any securities, shares, obligations or other interests of or in any organization, company or corporation which shall be from time to time held by my Canadian estate, to the same extent and as fully as I could if I were alive, and take up new or further shares, rights, obligations or other interests, join in plans for reconstruction or reorganization, exchange shares, rights, obligations or other interests, give, receive, accept and exercise options, and pay out of my Canadian estate any moneys which may be necessary for any of the purposes aforesaid.

11. ELECTIONS

My Canadian Trustee may, at any time and from time to time, make or not make any election, determination or designation, or do or not do any other act, deed or thing, or exercise any discretion or authority referred to in the *Income Tax Act*, R.S.C. 1985, c. 1 (5th Supp.), which my Canadian Trustee considers in the best interests of my Canadian estate and my beneficiaries or any of them.

VI. DEFINITION OF RELATIONSHIPS

Any reference in my Canadian Will or in any Codicil to a person in terms of a relationship to another person determined by blood or marriage shall not include a person born outside marriage or a person who comes within the description traced through another person who was born outside marriage. Any person who has been legally adopted shall be regarded as having been born in lawful wedlock to his or her adopting parent.

VII. EXCLUSIONS FROM NET FAMILY PROPERTY

I declare that the income, including capital gains, arising from any interest passing to a beneficiary under my Canadian Will shall be excluded from such beneficiary's net family property or from the value of the beneficiary's assets on the death, divorce or separation of such beneficiary, pursuant to the *Family Law Act*, R.S.O. 1990, c. F.3.

All gifts made, whether capital or revenue, shall be and remain the separate property of my beneficiaries and shall not fall into any Community of Property or be subject to any other matrimonial rights of the spouses of my beneficiaries and shall not be liable for the obligations of any such spouses or Community. All such gifts shall not be subject to seizure for the payment of any debts of beneficiaries or their representatives while in the possession and control of my Canadian Trustee.

VIII. COMPENSATION

I authorize my Canadian Trustee to take and transfer at reasonable intervals from the income and/or capital of my Canadian estate amounts on account of [his *or* her] compensation which my Canadian Trustee reasonably anticipates will be requested at the end of the accounting period in progress, either upon the audit of the Canadian estate accounts or on approval by the beneficiaries of my Canadian estate. If the amount subsequently awarded on Court audit or agreed to by the beneficiaries is less than the amount so taken, the excess shall be repaid to my Canadian estate without interest.

IX. GOVERNING LAW

My Canadian Will shall be governed by and construed in accordance with the laws of the Province of Ontario.

IN TESTIMONY WHEREOF I have to my Canadian Will, which is written upon this and preceding pages of paper, subscribed my name the day and year first above written.

SIGNED by the above-named)
Testator, as [his] Canadian)
Will, in the presence of us)
both, present at the same time,)
who at [his] request, in [his]) ____________
presence and in the presence of) [*Signature of testator*]
each other have subscribed our)
names as witnesses:)

Commentary: This precedent is effective to dispose of property which has its situs anywhere in Canada, but probate may be required in each province where property is found. This precedent was prepared for a German national whose only Ontario connection was real property in the province.

J-2 CERTIFICATE FOR INTERNATIONAL WILL.

Short description: Where a testator prepares separate wills for assets in several jurisdictions, this certificate is attached.

CERTIFICATE

1. I, , of the [City of Toronto], in the Province of Ontario, in the Dominion of Canada, solicitor, a person authorized to act in connection with international Wills,

2. Certify that on the day of , 19 , at [Toronto],

3. of the [City of Jerusalem], in the [State of Israel], in my presence and that of witnesses

4. (a) [*Name and address of witness*]
   (b) [*Name and address of witness*]
   has declared that the attached document is [his *or* her] Will and that [he *or* she] knows the contents thereof.

5. I furthermore certify that:
   (a) in my presence and in that of witnesses
      (i) the testator has signed the Will or has acknowledged [his *or* her] signature previously affixed.

6. The witnesses have signed the Will.

7. I have satisfied myself as to the identity of the testator and of the witnesses as designated above.

8. The witnesses met the conditions requisite to act as such according to the law under which I am acting.

Dated the day of , 19 , in the [City of Toronto], in the Province of Ontario, in the Dominion of Canada.

____

[*Signature of solicitor*]

Commentary: As previously mentioned, s. 42 of the *Succession Law Reform Act* provides for the international will. Section 42 contains a schedule setting out the requirements for the formal validity of an international will. The schedule creates designated persons who are authorized to act and to give the certificate which is the precedent here. In Ontario, this means all members of the Law Society except student members.

Sections 34 to 41 of the *Succession Law Reform Act* deal with conflict of laws, including the formal validity of wills and the rules for dispositions of personal and real property.

Chapter 5

CODICILS

I tend to avoid codicils in this era of word processing. A will's text is usually stored on disk, and so it is simpler to reprint the will, incorporating the necessary changes, than to prepare a codicil. A new will has the further advantage of not making it obvious to the beneficiaries whose gift is being dropped or reduced, as well as the advantage of avoiding transcription errors such as wrong paragraph numbers (see precedents K-3 and K-4).

For the client about to leave on an extended holiday, however, or for a very ill client, you may wish to consider dictating a holograph codicil for the client to write out as a quick alternative to formal documents.

K-1 SAMPLE CODICIL.

Short description: Like the sample will found in Chapter 2, this precedent is included solely to illustrate a whole codicil.

THE [FIRST] CODICIL

TO THE WILL

OF

[*Name of testator*]

[*Name of lawyer/law firm*]
Barristers & Solicitors
[*Address*]

THIS IS A [FIRST] CODICIL to the Will of me, , of the [City] of , in the [Municipality] of , and Province of Ontario, which Will is dated the day of , 19 .

1. I revoke Clause of my Will. I declare that the following clause numbered shall be inserted in its place, and shall have the same effect as if it had been originally inserted therein.

EXECUTOR AND TRUSTEE

I appoint my [husband], , to be the Executor and Trustee of my Will. If my [husband] does not survive me or is or becomes unwilling or unable to act as my Executor and Trustee before all the trusts set out in my Will have been fully performed, I appoint my [sister], , and the Trust Company to be the Executors and Trustees of my Will.

In my Will, I refer to the Executor and Trustee or Executors and Trustees, original or substituted or surviving, as my "Estate Trustee".

2. In all other respects I confirm my Will.

IN TESTIMONY WHEREOF I have to this [first] Codicil to my Will, which is written upon this and preceding pages of paper, subscribed my name on the day of , 19 .

SIGNED by as a [First] Codicil to [her] Will, in the presence of us both, present at the same time, who at [her] request, in [her] presence and in the presence of each other have subscribed our names as witnesses:	)	______________ *[Signature of testator]*
1. ______________ Signature of witness	)	
______________ Print name	)	
______________ Address	)	
______________ Occupation	)	
2. ______________ Signature of witness	)	
______________ Print name	)	
______________ Address	)	
______________ Occupation	)	

K-2 TITLE PAGE.

Short description: This is the introductory page to a codicil.

THE [FIRST] CODICIL

TO THE WILL

OF

[*Name of testator*]

[*Name of lawyer/law firm*]
Barrister & Solicitor
[*Address*]

Commentary: None.

K-3 INTRODUCTION.

Short description: The introduction identifies the codicil as being the first (or second or third as the case may be) codicil to the will of the testator.

> THIS IS A [FIRST] CODICIL to the Will of me, , of the [City] of , in the [Region] of , and Province of Ontario, which Will is dated the day of , 19 .

Commentary: The *Succession Law Reform Act*, R.S.O. 1990, c. S.26, s. 15, provides that:

> 15. A will or part of a will is revoked . . . by,
>
> . . . . .
>
> (c) a writing,
> (i) declaring an intention to revoke, and
> (ii) made in accordance with the provisions of [the Act] governing making of a will . . .

Hence, the codicil is an express revocation of or amendment to a previous testamentary document, usually a will, either in whole or in part. It must be made with the same statutory formalities which govern wills.

There are several problems which arise with codicils and, generally, because of word processing, I find it easier to re-create and revise the will as a whole rather than prepare a codicil.

Some of the problems with codicils are easily avoided and yet are commonplace occurrences. One is not ensuring that the names are the same from will to codicil to codicil. Then there is the problem of those transcribing wills often incorrectly setting out the date of the will in the text of the codicil. Typists are so used to typing the current year that they often type the current year instead of the year of the will. While these seem obvious matters, the fact that the same drafting errors keep happening is a reason for mentioning them.

Difficulties also arise when there is found a holograph document (that is, a document wholly in the handwriting of the testator) which appears to affect the provisions of an existing will. It is then a question of construction whether the holograph document is in fact a codicil. Reference may be made to *Coate Estate (Re)* (1987), 26 E.T.R. 161 (Ont. Surr. Ct.) and *Dixon-Marsden (Re)* (1985), 21 E.T.R. 216 (Ont. Surr. Ct.).

K-4 REVOCATION OF CLAUSES IN WILL.

Short description: The codicil directs revocation of specific clauses of a will, the new clauses are directed to be inserted and the balance of the will is confirmed.

> 1. I revoke Clause of my Will, such Clause beginning with the words " " and ending with the words " ". I declare that the following clause numbered shall be inserted in its place and shall have the same effect as if it had been originally inserted therein:
>
> [*New clause*]
>
> 2. In all other respects I confirm my Will.

Commentary: If you are revoking clauses of a will by referring to their paragraph numbers, make absolutely certain the paragraph numbers are correctly stated. It is fairly easy to transcribe a wrong number or to refer to the whole paragraph when it is only a subparagraph which is to be revoked.

Any part of the Will may be refused probate if it was inserted by mistake. However, the law is very strict about striking out passages of a will and inserting new paragraphs. A case which describes the futility of correcting mistakes, even though the mistake is obvious on all the evidence, is *Re Morris*, [1970] 1 All E.R. 1057 (P.D.A.).

K-5 ADDING CLAUSES TO WILL.

Short description: A clause is added to a will by the codicil.

1. I declare that the following Clause numbered shall be inserted in my Will immediately after Clause and shall have the same effect as if it had been originally inserted therein.

[*New clause*]

2. In all other respects I confirm my Will.

Commentary: A will may be amended by adding to it as well as by revoking and changing it. This precedent inserts a new clause and directs the place in the will where it is to be inserted. The place in the will can affect the interpretation and construction of the new clause, so it is appropriate to give this due consideration.

K-6 TESTIMONIUM.

Short description: The testator and the witnesses come together to execute the codicil.

IN TESTIMONY WHEREOF I have to this my [first] Codicil to my Will, which is written upon this and preceding pages of paper, subscribed my name the day and year first above written.

SIGNED by)
as a [first] Codicil to [her])
Will, in the presence of us)
both, present at the same)
time, who at [her] request,) ______________
in [her] presence and in the) [*Signature of testator*]
presence of each other have)

subscribed our names as)
witnesses:)
)
1. ______________________)
Signature of witness)
)
______________________)
Print name)
)
______________________)
Address)
)
______________________)
Occupation)
)
2. ______________________)
Signature of witness)
)
______________________)
Print name)
)
______________________)
Address)
)
______________________)
Occupation)

Commentary: See precedent M-3 for instructions for execution. The same formalities apply for execution of a codicil as a will.

Chapter 6

POWERS OF ATTORNEY FOR PROPERTY AND FOR PERSONAL CARE

In April, 1995, Ontario passed new legislation called the *Substitute Decisions Act, 1992*, S.O. 1992, c. 30, and three companion pieces of legislation. The *Substitute Decisions Act, 1992*, provided for financial powers of attorney and powers of attorney for personal care, and it also provided for those situations where someone becomes incapacitated but has not made such powers of attorney.

Immediately after the Act was passed, much alarm was expressed, particularly by senior citizens groups and other advocacy groups. Many articles appeared in the media which stated that, in the absence of proper powers of attorney, the management of our assets would be turned over to the government as we became incapacitated, and our family and friends would face a time-consuming and costly battle to gain control of our assets from the government.

As a result of public concern and a change in the government of Ontario, substantial amendments were made to the *Substitute Decisions Act, 1992*, by new legislation proclaimed in force on March 29, 1996.[1] This new legislation also repealed some of the companion legislation[2] and enacted a new *Health Care Consent Act, 1996*, S.O. 1996, c. 2, Sch. A. *Accordingly, commentaries and precedents written before March, 1996, should be regarded with caution.*

This chapter focuses on financial powers of attorney and powers of attorney for personal care, and will touch briefly on the roles of the Public Guardian and Trustee and of the court. The new legislation confirms that the Public Guardian and Trustee is the guardian of last resort rather than of first resort. This change was designed to meet the concerns of the media and the public about the difficulty

---

[1] *Advocacy, Consent and Substitute Decisions Statute Law Amendment Act, 1996*, S.O. 1996, c. 2.

[2] *Advocacy Act, 1992*, S.O. 1992, c. 26, repealed 1996, c. 2, s. 1; *Consent to Treatment Act, 1992*, S.O. 1992, c. 31, repealed *idem*, s. 2(2).

of planning in advance for the onset of incapacity and was made with a view to respecting and preserving the private arrangements of individuals.

1. *Continuing Powers of Attorney for Property*

Part I of the *Substitute Decisions Act, 1992* (the "Act"), dealing with property, applies to those who are at least 18 years old (s. 4) and are incapable of managing property. A person will be considered incapable of managing property if he or she is unable to understand information relevant to making a decision about the management of property, or if he or she is not able to appreciate the reasonably foreseeable consequences of a decision or lack of decision (s. 6). Decisions on behalf of such incapacitated people may be made by:

(a) an attorney under a continuing power of attorney;
(b) a statutory guardian; or
(c) a court-appointed guardian.

Part I of the Act addresses in great detail when someone (the "grantor") will be capable of giving a continuing power of attorney for property (s. 8). A person may do so if he or she:

(a) knows what kind of property he or she has and its approximate value;
(b) is aware of obligations to dependants;
(c) knows what his or her attorney will have the authority to do;
(d) knows that the attorney must account for his or her dealings with the property;
(e) knows that, if capable, he or she may revoke the power of attorney;
(f) appreciates that unless the attorney manages the property prudently, its value may deteriorate; and
(g) appreciates the possibility that the attorney could misuse the authority given by the power of attorney.

Section 10[3] of the Act continues the requirement for *two* witnesses. There is a short list of people who cannot be witnesses, including the attorney or the attorney's spouse or partner, the grantor's spouse or partner, a child of the grantor or a person towards whom the grantor has demonstrated a settled intention to treat as his or her child, a person whose property is under guardianship or who has a guardian of

[3] Amended 1996, c. 2, s. 6.

the person, and a person under 18. The previous legislation required a statement by the witnesses to the effect that they had no reason to believe the person giving the power of attorney was incapable at the time. Such a statement is no longer required.

Attorneys who wish to resign should refer to s. 11[4] of the Act. They no longer need to notify the Office of the Public Guardian and Trustee. It is sufficient for the resignation to be effective if a copy of it is delivered to the grantor, the other attorneys under the document, the substitute if one is named by the document, the spouse or partner, and certain relatives. If the grantor and his or her spouse are living separate and apart, there are exceptions to giving notice to the spouse of the grantor and to the relatives who are related only by marriage (s. 11(1.1)).[5] Both "partner" and "relatives" are defined by s. 1 of the Act. Partners, for all purposes of the Act, are people who "have lived together for at least one year and have a close personal relationship that is of primary importance in both persons' lives" (s. 1(2)). People are relatives, for all purposes of the Act, if they are related by blood, marriage or adoption (s. 1(2.1)).[6] Finally, s. 11(2)[7] requires the attorney who wishes to resign to make reasonable efforts to give notice to those with whom he or she was dealing on behalf of the grantor and with whom further dealings are likely to be required on behalf of the grantor.

The continuing power of attorney can be terminated in a number of different ways. Section 12[8] provides that termination will occur in the following circumstances:

(1) The attorney dies, becomes incapable of managing property or resigns, unless there is another attorney authorized to act or there is a substitution created by the power of attorney.
(2) The court appoints a guardian of the property of the grantor.
(3) The grantor executes a new continuing power of attorney for property (unless there are to be multiple powers of attorney).
(4) The power of attorney is revoked.
(5) The grantor dies.

A revocation must be in writing and must be executed in the same way as a continuing power of attorney for property (s. 12(2)). Like previous powers of attorney legislation in Ontario, third parties

[4] Amended *idem*, s. 7.
[5] Enacted *idem*, s. 7(2).
[6] Enacted *idem*, s. 3(6).
[7] Enacted *idem*, s. 7(3).
[8] Amended *idem*, s. 8.

acting in good faith and without knowledge of the termination of a continuing power of attorney for property or its invalidity are protected by any subsequent exercise of power by the attorney (s. 13(1)).

Finally, s. 14 deems powers of attorney executed previous to October 3, 1995, to be continuing powers of attorney for property pursuant to the Act if they expressly state that they may be used during a subsequent legal incapacity of the grantor, as provided in s. 5[9] of the *Powers of Attorney Act*, R.S.O. 1990, c. P.20, if they were executed in accordance with that Act, and if they are otherwise valid.

Prior to the March, 1996, amendments, the most troubling sections of the *Substitute Decisions Act, 1992*, were ss. 15 to 21,[10] which created statutory guardianship of a person's property by the Public Guardian and Trustee and others in certain circumstances. The March, 1996, amendments ensure that where there is a continuing power of attorney for property, it will take precedence over appointment of the Public Guardian and Trustee as the statutory guardian. Continuing powers of attorney for property which cover all of the grantor's property cannot now be terminated by appointment of the Office of the Public Guardian and Trustee.

Section 17[11] of the Act lists the people who may apply to the Public Guardian and Trustee to replace him or her as statutory guardian. They include the incapable person's spouse or partner, a relative of the incapable person, the incapable person's attorney under a continuing power of attorney which does not give the attorney authority over all the incapable person's property, and a trust company if the spouse or partner consents.

The Act preserves the right of the court, on application, to appoint a guardian of property for a person incapable of managing property where it is necessary for decisions to be made on his or her behalf. In keeping with the March, 1996, amendments, s. 24[12] ensures that the Public Guardian and Trustee will not be appointed unless there is no suitable person available and willing to be appointed. "Suitable" is not defined.

The Act creates all the powers and duties of a guardian of property and an attorney under a continuing power of attorney. (The document itself may modify these powers.) It is useful to review some of

---

[9] Repealed 1992, c. 32, s. 24(3).

[10] Section 15 amended 1996, c. 2, s. 9; s. 16 repealed and substituted *idem*, s. 10; s. 16.1 enacted *idem*; s. 17 repealed and substituted *idem*, s. 11; s. 18 amended *idem*, s. 12; ss. 19 and 20 repealed and substituted *idem*, s. 13; ss. 20.1 to 20.3 enacted *idem*.

[11] Repealed and substituted *idem*, s. 11.

[12] Amended *idem*, s. 14.

the statutory powers and the general principles which are expressed in the Act. The reader is referred to ss. 31 to 42.[13] While these sections refer only to guardians of property, s. 38[14] provides that attorneys under continuing powers of attorney for property generally speaking have the same powers and duties.

The guardian or attorney has power by s. 31(1) to do on behalf of an incapable person "anything in respect of property" that the incapable person could do if capable, except make a will. Such a power of attorney is intended for the management of "property", which is not defined. However, it is clear that the attorney is authorized to deal with financial issues arising out of the property of the grantor. There are thus many areas where the attorney cannot act. For example, the attorney may not fulfil the fiduciary obligations of the grantor if the grantor was active as the executor and trustee of a third party.

The legislation specifically addresses the making of wills. An attorney cannot make a will for the grantor even though a will relates to the "property" of the grantor.

Section 32[15] sets out other powers and duties of the guardian or attorney:

(1) The guardian or attorney must explain to the incapable person what the guardian's powers and duties are.
(2) The guardian or attorney must encourage the incapable person to participate to the best of his or her abilities in the guardian's decisions.
(3) The guardian or attorney must foster regular contact between the incapable person and supportive family members and friends, and he or she must consult with those people and with the attorney for personal care.
(4) The guardian or attorney must keep accounts of all transactions as required by the regulations.
(5) A different standard of care is created for attorneys and guardians who are compensated as opposed to those who are not compensated. Those who receive compensation are held to the standard of care, diligence and skill that a person in the business of managing the property of others is required to exercise.

---

[13] Section 31 amended *idem*, s. 19; s. 32 amended *idem*, s. 20; ss. 33.1 and 33.2 enacted *idem*, s. 21; s. 35.1 enacted *idem*, s. 22; s. 36 repealed and substituted *idem*, s. 23; s. 36.1 enacted 1994, c. 27, s. 62(2); s. 37 amended 1996, c. 2, s. 24; s. 38 amended *idem*, s. 25; s. 39 repealed and substituted *idem*, s. 26; s. 40 amended *idem*, s. 27; s. 41 repealed *idem*, s. 28; s. 42 amended 1994, c. 27, s. 43(2).

[14] Amended 1996, c. 2, s. 25.

[15] Amended *idem*, s. 20.

6. If a management plan is in place, the guardian for property must act in accordance with that plan and its amendments.

Under s. 32, guardians and attorneys are fiduciaries and must exercise their powers and duties diligently, with honesty and integrity, in good faith and for the incapable person's benefit. This is an important addition because the common law has been unclear as to whether attorneys are fiduciaries or merely agents. It is important to note that the guardian or attorney must make decisions regarding the incapable person's property which are consistent with decisions concerning that person's personal care which are made by the attorney or guardian for personal care. It would appear that this requirement gives precedence to the power of attorney for personal care or to the court-appointed guardian of the person.

The Act makes it clear that a guardian of property and an attorney must make reasonable efforts to determine whether an incapable person has a will and, if so, what the provisions of that will are. Accordingly, s. 33.2[16] provides that property in the control of a third person must be turned over to the attorney or guardian, and it specifically states that such property includes the incapable person's will.

Section 35.1[17] provides that neither the guardian of property nor the attorney shall dispose of property that the guardian or attorney knows is subject to a specific testamentary gift. The single exception is a testamentary gift of money. Despite this exception, the guardian may dispose of property if the disposition is necessary to comply with his or her duties, and the guardian may make a gift of property to a person who would be entitled to it under the incapable person's will if the gift is authorized by s. 37[18] of the Act. A guardian or attorney who is aware of dispositions under an incapable person's will should review very carefully the provisions of ss. 35.1[19] and 36[20] in order to ensure that any actions taken in accordance with the provisions of the will are correctly carried out. The scope of this work does not permit a detailed inquiry into these sections.

Section 37(1) sets out required expenditures. These expenditures include those that are reasonably necessary for the incapable person's support, care and education, those that are reasonably necessary for the support, care and education of that person's dependants, and those that are necessary to satisfy the person's other legal obligations. Sec-

[16] Enacted *idem*, s. 21.
[17] Enacted *idem*, s. 22.
[18] Amended *idem*, s. 24.
[19] Enacted *idem*, s. 22.
[20] Repealed and substituted *idem*, s. 23.

tion 37(2) creates principles to guide the attorney in making such expenditures.

Section 37(3) lists optional expenditures, being gifts or loans to an incapable person's friends and relatives and charitable gifts. Section 37(4) creates guiding principles for these expenditures.

2. *Continuing Powers of Attorney for Personal Care*

Part II of the *Substitute Decisions Act, 1992*, deals with powers of attorney for the person. Until this Act was proclaimed in April, 1995, any authority given to another person to make personal care decisions and to give consents to health care had no legal validity and was regarded merely as an expression of intention. Part II of the Act authorizes the making, use, termination and revocation of powers of attorney for personal care, it provides for court-appointed guardians of the person, and it sets out the duties of the guardian and the attorney for personal care.

Section 46[21] of the Act allows the grantor, provided he or she is capable, to make a power of attorney for personal care. This authorizes an attorney to make decisions on the grantor's behalf with respect to health care, nutrition, shelter, clothing, hygiene or safety. The grantor will be considered capable if he or she has the ability to understand whether or not the proposed attorney has a genuine concern for his or her welfare and appreciates that he or she may need to have the attorney make decisions (s. 47(1)). Note that this is a much lower standard than that required for making a continuing power of attorney for property. The attorney for personal care may be the Public Guardian and Trustee (s. 46(2)).[22] The attorney shall not be someone who provides health care to the grantor for compensation or who provides residential, social, training or support services to the grantor for compensation, unless the attorney is also the spouse, partner or relative of the grantor (s. 46(3)).[23]

People making powers of attorney often ask if it is possible to have more than one attorney. Section 46(4) provides that two or more attorneys may be appointed and shall act jointly unless the grantor provides otherwise. If one of the joint appointees dies, becomes incapable or resigns, the remaining attorneys are authorized to act unless the document itself provides otherwise.

---

[21] Amended *idem*, s. 30.
[22] Repealed and substituted *idem*, s. 30(1).
[23] Amended *idem*, s. 30(3).

Like the continuing power of attorney for property, a power of attorney for personal care must be executed in the presence of two witnesses (s. 48(1)).[24] The same class of people set out in s. 10(2) who cannot be witnesses to a continuing power of attorney for property also cannot be witnesses to a continuing power of attorney for personal care (s. 48(2)). Previous legislation required the witnesses to state that they had no reason to believe that the grantor was incapable of giving the power of attorney for personal care. This is no longer a requirement.

You should note at the outset that the attorney has no authority to act under a continuing power of attorney for personal care *unless* the grantor is incapable. Section 45 provides that a person is incapable of personal care "if the person is not able to understand information that is relevant to making a decision concerning his or her own health care, nutrition, shelter, clothing, hygiene or safety, or is not able to appreciate the reasonably foreseeable consequences of a decision or lack of decision".

Prior to the March, 1996, amendments, an attorney was authorized to make a decision when he or she had reasonable grounds to believe that the grantor was incapable of making the decision and the grantor did not object after the attorney had explained the necessity for the decision. If the grantor objected, the attorney could not make the decision until the power of attorney was validated, a process designed to confirm that the grantor was incapable. This process required application to the Public Guardian and Trustee for validation, an assessment by two assessors confirming incapacity, and an advocate to give rights advice and confirm that the grantor did not object to the validation.

The March, 1996, amendments repealed the right of the grantor to object to an attorney's decision, and it repealed the necessity of the validation process. Under the amendments the attorney for personal care is authorized to make a decision concerning the grantor's personal care if:

(a) the *Health Care Consent Act, 1996*, applies to the decision, and the grantor is sound and capable under that legislation;
(b) the *Health Care Consent Act, 1996*, does not apply, but the attorney has reasonable grounds to believe that the grantor is incapable of making the decision, unless there is a condition in the power of attorney which prevents the attorney from making such a decision until incapacity is confirmed (s. 49(1)).[25]

---

[24] Repealed and substituted *idem*, s. 31(1).
[25] Repealed and substituted *idem*, s. 32(1).

Under s. 47(4) of the Act, instructions contained in a power of attorney for personal care with respect to a decision the attorney is authorized to make are valid if, at the time the power of attorney was executed, the grantor had the capacity to make that decision for him or herself.

The powers of the attorney may be restricted by the grantor. Most of my clients want conditions and restrictions which are really expressions of intention and are similar to the provisions created in a living will (precedent L-6) or directive for health care (precedent L-5). However, it is also possible for the power of attorney to be very specific about particular care, medical procedures, treatments, etc. If your client is interested in extensive conditions and restrictions, I would recommend that he or she review these with his or her family physician, since the lawyer preparing the document can be on uncertain ground in the medical world. You and your clients might want to get in touch with the University of Toronto Centre for Bioethics, which has documents suitable for these more extensive decisions with respect to health and personal care. The Centre for Bioethics is located at:

88 College Street
Toronto
Ontario M5G 1L4
Tel.: (416) 978-2709

Thus you can see that the power of attorney for personal care need not be in any particular form, although there is a prescribed form.

If the attorney wants to resign, s. 52[26] sets out the requirements. There is nothing in the Act which prevents an attorney from resigning. However, the resignation is not effective unless it is delivered to:

(a) the grantor;
(b) any other attorney under the power of attorney;
(c) the substitute attorney if one is named; and
(d) the grantor's spouse or partner and the relatives who are known to the attorney and who reside in Ontario unless the power of attorney says that this is not necessary.

If the grantor and his or her spouse are living separate and apart, the amended Act no longer requires that the notice be given to the spouse or to the relatives of the spouse. The attorney is to make reasonable efforts to give notice of the resignation to those with whom the attorney was previously dealing and with whom further dealings are likely to be required on behalf of the grantor.

[26] Amended *idem*, s. 33.

Under s. 53(1),[27] the death of the attorney or his or her becoming incapable or resigning terminates the power of attorney unless another person is authorized to act or the power of attorney provides for a substitution. The power of attorney is also terminated if the court appoints a guardian for the grantor, if the grantor executes a new power of attorney for personal care (unless there are multiple powers of attorney for personal care), or if the grantor revokes the power of attorney. Under s. 47(3) of the Act, a person is capable of revoking his or her power of attorney for personal care if he or she is capable of giving such a power of attorney. The revocation must be in writing and executed in the same way as the power of attorney for personal care (s. 53(2)).

Sections 55 to 65[28] of the Act provide for court-appointed guardians of the person. The court may, on any person's application, appoint a guardian for a person who is not capable of personal care and who, as a result, needs decisions to be made for him or her (s. 55(1)). In keeping with the intent of the March, 1996, amendments, the Public Guardian and Trustee shall not be appointed as a guardian unless the application proposes the Public Guardian and Trustee and there is no other suitable person available and willing to be appointed (s. 57(2.2)).[29] Again, "suitable" is not defined. As well, a health care provider who receives compensation is not to be appointed unless he or she is the incapable person's spouse, partner or relative (s. 57(1))[30] and (2).

The order of the court appointing a guardian must contain a finding that the person:

(a) is incapable because he or she is not able to understand information relevant to making a decision concerning health care, nutrition, shelter, clothing, hygiene or safety;
(b) is not able to appreciate the reasonably foreseeable consequences of the decision or lack of a decision, and in consequence needs to have the decision made for him or her (s. 58(1)).

The guardianship may be limited to a particular period and may impose any other conditions which the court considers appropriate (s. 58(2)).

[27] Amended *idem*, s. 34(1) and (2).
[28] Section 57 amended *idem*, s. 36; s. 59 amended *idem*, s. 37; s. 60 amended *idem*, s. 38; s. 61 repealed and substituted *idem*, s. 39; s. 62 amended *idem*, s. 40; ss. 63 and 64 repealed and substituted *idem*, s. 41; s. 65 amended *idem*, s. 42.
[29] Enacted *idem*, s. 36(3).
[30] Amended *idem*, s. 36(2).

The Act also provides for substitution of another person as guardian (s. 61).[31]

A court-appointed guardian has the powers set out in s. 59(2),[32] which are:

(a) exercising custodial power, including determining living arrangements and providing for safety and shelter;
(b) being the person's litigation guardian, except with respect to litigation that relates to the person's property or the guardian's status or powers;
(c) settling claims and commencing and settling proceedings on the incapable person's behalf, except those claims and proceedings relating to property or the guardian's status or powers;
(d) gaining access to personal information, including health information and records, except for the purposes of litigation relating to property or the guardian's status or powers;
(e) making any decision to which the *Health Care Consent Act, 1996*, applies;
(f) making decisions about health care, nutrition and hygiene;
(g) making decisions about the person's employment, education, training, clothing, recreation and social services delivery;
(h) exercising any other powers and performing any other duties specified in the order.

Section 61[33] provides for variation of the court order appointing the guardian.

Finally, ss. 66 to 68[34] of the Act provide for the duties of guardians of the person and attorneys for personal care. These sections begin with a general statement that the powers and duties of the guardian are to be exercised and performed diligently and in good faith. The guardian is also to explain to the incapable person what the guardian's duties and powers are.

The guardian may make any decisions to which the *Health Care Consent Act, 1996*, applies (s. 66(2.1)).[35] For decisions to which the *Health Care Consent Act, 1996*, does not apply, the following are given as guiding principles (s. 66(3)):[36]

---

[31] Repealed and substituted *idem*, s. 39.
[32] Amended *idem*, s. 37(1).
[33] Repealed and substituted *idem*, s. 39.
[34] Section 66 amended *idem*, s. 43; ss. 67 and 68 repealed and substituted *idem*, s. 44.
[35] Enacted *idem*, s. 43(1).
[36] Amended *idem*, s. 43(2).

(1) If the guardian knows of a wish or instruction applicable to the circumstances of the incapable person which the incapable person made while capable, the guardian shall make the decision in accordance with that wish or instruction.
(2) The guardian shall use reasonable diligence in ascertaining whether there are such wishes or instructions.
(3) A later wish or instruction expressed while capable prevails over an earlier wish or instruction.
(4) If the guardian does not know of a wish or instruction, or if it is impossible to make the decision in accordance with the wish or instruction, the guardian shall make the decision in the incapable person's best interests.

With regard to guideline (4), the legislation sets out the things which the guardian is to take into consideration in determining the "best interests" of the incapable person (s. 66(4)).[37] These include:

(a) the values and beliefs that the guardian knows were held by the person while capable;
(b) the person's current wishes if ascertainable;
(c) whether the decision will improve the quality of the person's life, prevent the quality of his or her life from deteriorating, or reduce the extent to which, or the rate at which, the quality of the person's life is likely to deteriorate; and
(d) whether the benefit to the person will outweigh the harm from any other decision.

An attorney for personal care and a guardian of the person may at any time have resort to the court for directions on any question arising in the guardianship or under the power of attorney (s. 68(1)).[38] This may be done by way of application, or by motion in the context of a proceeding already commenced (s. 68(2)).[39]

3. *Procedure in Guardianship Applications*

This book is not intended to review the procedure in guardianship applications. Although there can be many problems arising out of the preparation and use of powers of attorney for personal care and powers of attorney for property, I recommend that these documents be made as part of the planning process to ensure that people plan for their

[37] Repealed and substituted *idem*, s. 43(3).
[38] Repealed and substituted *idem*, s. 44.
[39] Repealed and substituted *idem*.

incapacity in the same way that they plan for their estates, with the result that guardianship applications will not be necessary. If court applications are required, the reader is directed to Part III of the Act and to the regulations.

4. *Health Care Consent Act, 1996*

The *Health Care Consent Act, 1996*, is relevant to substitute decision-making on behalf of people who are not capable of deciding about "treatment". Treatment is defined by s. 2(1) of that Act as anything done for a therapeutic, preventative, palliative, diagnostic, cosmetic or other health-related purpose, and includes a course or plan of treatment. There are several exceptions which should be referred to.

By s. 4(2), a person is presumed to be capable with respect to treatment, admission to a care facility and personal assistance services. By s. 4(3), anyone is entitled to rely on the presumption of capacity with respect to another person unless he or she has reasonable grounds to believe that the other person is incapable with respect to the treatment, the admission or the personal assistance service. No treatment can be provided without the consent of a capable person, or if the person is not capable, without the consent of the person's substitute decision-maker.

You are able, while capable, to express wishes about treatment, admission to a care facility or a personal assistance service. This may be done in a power of attorney as previously discussed, in a prescribed form, orally or in some other manner (s. 5).

The *Health Care Consent Act, 1996*, greatly assists in any situation where an incapable person should be receiving treatment. Section 20(1) creates a rank of people who can make substitute decisions about treatment. In keeping with the intent of this Act and the *Substitute Decisions Act, 1992*, the guardian of the person is ranked first. The attorney for personal care is ranked second. Thereafter, the ranking is as follows:

(a) the person's personal representative who is appointed by the Consent and Capacity Board;
(b) the person's spouse or partner (unless separated);
(c) a child or parent of the incapable person (not including a parent who only has a right of access), or the Children's Aid Society or other person lawfully entitled to deal with consent in the place of the parent;

(d) a parent who has only a right of access, a brother, a sister, or any other relative.

Not surprisingly, any substitute decision-maker must be at least 16 years of age, available, willing to give consent, capable of making a decision with respect to treatment for him or herself, and not prohibited by the court or by a separation agreement from having access to the incapable person or giving consent (s. 20(2)).

Section 21 creates principles for giving or refusing consent on behalf of an incapable person:

(1) If the person knows of a wish expressed by the incapable person while capable and after age 16, the person shall give or refuse consent in accordance with that wish.
(2) If the person does not know of such a wish, or if it is impossible to comply with a wish made, the person shall act in the best interests of the incapable person. "Best interests" is defined in s. 21(2). If you are advising clients who are required to give consent, you and your clients should review this definition.

L-1 CONTINUING POWER OF ATTORNEY FOR PROPERTY.

Short description: This precedent is a general continuing power of attorney for property. The power of attorney need not be in this form to be effective.

CONTINUING POWER OF ATTORNEY FOR PROPERTY

THIS CONTINUING POWER OF ATTORNEY FOR PROPERTY is made by , of the City of , in the Municipality of .

APPOINTMENT

1. I APPOINT to be my attorney for property. I authorize my attorney to do, on my behalf,

any acts which I can do by an attorney, and specifically anything in respect of property that I could do if capable of managing property, subject to any conditions or restrictions contained in this Continuing Power of Attorney for Property.

POWER TO MANAGE PROPERTY

2. This document is a continuing power of attorney for property under the *Substitute Decisions Act, 1992*, S.O. 1992, c. 30, as amended, and may be used during my incapacity to manage property.

EFFECTIVE DATE

3. This Continuing Power of Attorney comes into effect on the date it is signed and witnessed.

CONDITIONS AND RESTRICTIONS

4. [*List conditions and restrictions.*]

REVOCATION

5. I revoke any prior Continuing Power of Attorney for Property given by me.

MULTIPLE POWERS OF ATTORNEY

6. I retain the right to make multiple Continuing Powers of Attorney for Property

DELEGATION

7. I authorize my attorney to delegate my attorney's authority to some other person and to revoke or suspend such delegation.

FAMILY LAW ACT CONSENT

8. I authorize my attorney named to exercise all of my rights with respect to the disposition, encumbrance or possession of a matrimonial home under

the *Family Law Act*, R.S.O. 1990, c. F.3, whether or not my name appears on the title, including consenting to any disposition or encumbrance by my spouse of any interest in our matrimonial home.

Obligations to Others

9. My attorney for property may manage my estate for my benefit, for the benefit of any other person, including my attorney, to fulfil any legal obligation I may have.

Litigation Guardian

10. My attorney shall have the authority to act as my litigation guardian if one is required to commence, defend or represent me in any court proceedings.

Compensation

11. I authorize my attorney for property to take annual compensation from my property in accordance with the fee scale prescribed by regulation for the compensation of guardians of property made pursuant to Sections 40(1) and 90 of the *Substitute Decisions Act, 1992*, as amended.

Revenue Canada

12. My attorney for property is my "legal representative" for all purposes of the *Income Tax Act*, R.S.C. 1985, c. 1 (5th Supp.), with respect to any dealings with the Government of Canada, or any institution controlled by the Government of Canada.

Witnesses

13. We have signed this power of attorney in the presence of the person whose name appears above and in the presence of each other.

14. SIGNED BY:______________________________
on the day of , 19 , in the presence of the witnesses whose names appear below, and who signed on the same date.

________________________)
Witness)
)
________________________)
Print name and address)
)
________________________)
)
)
)
________________________)
Witness)
)
________________________)
Print name and address)
)
________________________)

Commentary: A power of attorney is a written authorization given by one person (the donor) to another (the attorney), empowering the attorney to do legal acts on behalf of the donor that the donor could do for him or herself. The giving of a power of attorney does not take away the donor's power to act on his or her own behalf; it merely authorizes the attorney to share that power.

A power of attorney may be general and contain no conditions or restrictions, or it may be restricted as to the powers being shared, the term to which it applies, etc.

The attorney will continue to exercise power during any subsequent incapacity of the donor if the power of attorney so indicates. If this provision is not present, an incapacity revokes the power of attorney. If this clause is inserted, the power of attorney survives the incapacity; hence it is referred to as a "continuing" power of attorney.

As a practical matter, I do not usually draft the power of attorney to allow for a substitute attorney in the event of a contingency such as the first named attorney becoming incapacitated. It can be impossible for the substitute to prove he or she is entitled to exercise the power because that would involve proving the incapacity on an ongoing basis. The bank teller, for example, could quite properly ask for proof that "Mrs. X is incapacitated today". One solution to this problem is to reconsider the appointment and name the substitute and the named attorney to act together, *jointly* or *jointly and severally*. If that is not desirable, an alternative is to create two powers of attorney, taking care that one does not revoke the other, and to enter into an understanding with the attorneys as to when the substitute may act. This has little legal comfort since the attorney named in the second document can act immediately if he or she decides to do so; thus, in this kind of situation, a firm understanding among trusted friends and family is essential.

L-2 MEMORANDUM OF INTENT.

Short description: This is a companion document to the continuing power of attorney for property, and is used where the donor wishes some guidelines on the use of the power. The following is a sample memorandum. The editor gratefully acknowledges the personal trust staff of the Canada Trust Company in Toronto for providing this memorandum.

LETTER OF INTENT

Regarding the Continuing Power of Attorney for Property dated   , 19   , a copy of which is attached hereto (the "Power of Attorney"):

To: The Canada Trust Company ("Canada Trust")

From:

Canada Trust agrees to act under the Power of Attorney in the event:

(a) I direct Canada Trust, in writing, to commence to act under the Power of Attorney; or
(b) A qualified medical doctor, acting on my behalf, advises Canada Trust, in writing, that in his or her opinion, it would be unwise for me to continue to independently handle my own financial affairs, or words to that effect; or
(c) Canada Trust, in its discretion, based on information available to it, may determine that it would be in my best financial interest for Canada Trust to commence to act under the Power of Attorney, in the event that I am unable to give directions under (a) above, and Canada Trust is unable to obtain an opinion from a medical doctor as in (b) above.

If Canada Trust is acting as my attorney in accordance with the powers granted to it under the Power of Attorney, Canada Trust may:

1. Retain, manage, reinvest, sell or in any way deal as Canada Trust considers appropriate with any of my property and enter into any obligation associated with such property as it considers appropriate. In making any investments, Canada Trust may make such investments as it shall think appropriate without being limited to investments authorized by law for trustees. Without limiting the generality of the foregoing, I specifically authorize Canada Trust to invest in any mutual funds or pooled investments, including one or more of the Common Trust Funds and/or Everest Funds managed and/or operated by Canada Trust and/or its related companies. Canada Trust may open in my name a managed agency account operated by Canada Trust (currently known as an Investment Management Account). Canada Trust may administer the said account in accordance with the terms and conditions contained in the Investment Account in effect from time to time and with such service selections as Canada Trust may select on my behalf.
2. Manage my property so that so much of the

income and/or capital as Canada Trust considers appropriate shall be applied for my care, maintenance and general benefit. Canada Trust may pay any of my medical or nursing expenses that may be necessary, and provide funds for any benefits including clothing or comforts that may be properly required by me.

(*N.B. Paragraphs 2(a) and 2(b) are optional.*)

2(a) In the event that I have not appointed an attorney for personal care, I request Canada Trust to make any personal decisions for me that I am incapable of making for myself including choice of accommodation, hiring a nurse or companion to attend to my personal care and expenditures for my care and comfort, but excluding decisions concerning medical treatment or the giving or refusing of consent to treatment.

2(b) I acknowledge that Canada Trust cannot participate in any decision concerning my medical treatment; however, when I am no longer capable of making decisions myself, I request that Canada Trust deliver to my physician, , or the attending physician at any institution in which I may be resident, the advance directive concerning medical treatment dated which has been filed with the Power of Attorney and Letter of Intent.

3. Secure and act upon the opinion or advice of, or information obtained from, any lawyer, accountant, financial advisor, broker, investment counsellor, auctioneer, surveyor, valuer, life or fire insurance advisor, or other expert and pay their reasonable expenses.

4. Dispose of any of my household items if, in the discretion of Canada Trust, it shall become necessary. Such items shall be disposed, to the extent that it is practical in the opinion of Canada Trust, in accordance with any memorandum which I may have prepared or any instructions which are contained in my will. I acknowledge

that I have been advised and am aware that my will is not valid until my death. In the event that no executed will or memorandum or copies of such documents or notes relating to such documents can be located, or in the event that Canada Trust shall be unable to attain access to such documents, my household items may be disposed of in such manner as Canada Trust, in its discretion, shall deem advisable.

(*N.B. Paragraphs 5, 6 and 7 are optional.*)

5. Canada Trust may manage my assets:
   — for my benefit;
   — for the benefit of any person to whom I am under legal obligation to provide a benefit, to the extent Canada Trust considers it necessary to fulfil such obligation;
   — for the benefit of any charitable purpose or any person Canada Trust considers I would have wished to benefit were I acting personally instead of by my attorney.

6. I further direct that Canada Trust shall consult with in all matters of importance relating to my financial affairs and provide with regular statements of the financial transactions made on my behalf.

7. I acknowledge that the fees referred to in clause 4(c) of the Power of Attorney are the fees of Canada Trust and that any fees to be paid to have been agreed separately with in a document/letter dated , a copy of which is attached to this Letter of Intent.

Canada Trust shall not be held responsible for any loss to my property resulting from an exercise of its discretion under the Power of Attorney done in good faith.

Dated this __________ day of __________, 1996

______________________	______________________
Signature of Witness	Signature of Grantor

Commentary: An attorney is a fiduciary and would not be entitled to remuneration unless this were dealt with by provincial legislation.

L-3 CONTINUING POWER OF ATTORNEY FOR PROPERTY — VARIATION.

Short description: This is a variation of precedent L-1. The client gives to a chosen attorney the power to make any type of decision about his or her property, pursuant to the *Substitute Decisions Act, 1992*. The author once again thanks the Canada Trust Company for this precedent.

CONTINUING POWER OF ATTORNEY FOR PROPERTY MADE IN ACCORDANCE WITH THE SUBSTITUTE DECISIONS ACT, 1992, S.O. 1992, c. 30

This continuing power of attorney for property is given by of the of in the Province of Ontario.

(*Delete inapplicable clause 1.*)

1. I revoke any continuing power of attorney for property previously given by me.

1. I revoke any continuing power of attorney for property previously given by me, with the exception of:

2. I appoint The Canada Trust Company (''Canada Trust'') and of jointly to be my attorneys for property and I authorize my attorneys to do on my behalf anything in respect of property that I could do if capable of managing property, except make a will, subject to the law

and any conditions or restrictions contained in this document. I direct that my attorney, Canada Trust, shall assume the burden of the administration and shall keep in its custody all of my assets.

3. It is my intention that this document is a continuing power of attorney for property pursuant to the *Substitute Decisions Act, 1992* and may be used during my incapacity to manage property.

4. This power of attorney includes the following powers:
   (a) I authorize my attorneys to exercise all such powers in my name as I would be able to exercise had I chosen to exercise such powers myself, or had I legal capacity to exercise such powers. This therefore authorizes my attorneys to bind and secure information on behalf of my assets in respect of their dealings with any person. Without restricting the generality of the foregoing, I expressly constitute my attorneys as my "legal representative" for the purposes of s. 150(1)(d) and all other purposes of the *Income Tax Act* (Canada), and authorize my attorneys to bind and secure information on behalf of my assets in respect of any matter involving the government of Canada or any institution, such as a bank, regulated by the government of Canada.
   (b) I authorize my attorneys to delegate any act my attorneys may exercise to some other person, and to revoke or suspend such delegation.
   (c) I authorize my attorney, Canada Trust, to receive and draw on an interim basis from my assets the fees, reimbursement and other compensation which shall be calculated in accordance with the prescribed fee structure of Canada Trust in effect from time to time for a managed agency account, currently known as an Investment Account. For other services, my attorney Canada Trust shall be entitled to charge on a time charge basis at its usual hourly rate or rates from time to time. It is

understood that there will be no charge for holding this power of attorney so long as my attorneys do not act under it.

(d) I authorize my attorneys to take physical possession of all my property, including property held in a safety deposit box, property held in safekeeping by others on my behalf, and property held by others subject to some professional privilege, which privilege I waive for this purpose. For greater certainty, my attorneys shall be entitled to review my will, in order to be able to manage my assets in a manner that is sensitive thereto.

(e) I authorize my attorneys to provide any consent on my behalf with respect to any right of possession or other interest I may have in a matrimonial home under the *Family Law Act*.

(f) I authorize my attorneys to make any beneficiary designation that I would be entitled to make in any registered retirement savings plan or registered retirement income fund owned by me.

5. In making this power of attorney, I am aware:
   — of the nature and extent of my property;
   — of the obligations I owe to my dependants;
   — that my attorneys will be able to do on my behalf anything in respect of property that I could do if capable, except make a will, except to the extent that the power of attorney sets out conditions and restrictions on the powers of my attorneys;
   — that my attorneys must account for their dealings with my property;
   — that I may, while capable, revoke the power of attorney;
   — that the value of my property administered by my attorneys may decline unless my attorneys manage it prudently;
   — that there is a possibility that my attorneys could misuse the authority given to my attorneys by the power of attorney.

6. This continuing power of attorney will come into effect on the date it is signed and witnessed.

I have signed this power of attorney in the presence of both the witnesses whose names appear below.

I HAVE SIGNED THIS
POWER OF ATTORNEY ON ____________________
Date

____
Signature

We are the witnesses to this power of attorney. We have signed this power of attorney in the presence of the person whose name appears above, and in the presence of each other, on the date shown above. Neither one of us is the attorney, a spouse or partner of the attorney, a spouse or child of the grantor or person whom the grantor has demonstrated a settled intention to treat as a child of the grantor, a person whose property is under guardianship or who has a guardian of the person, or less than eighteen years old.

Witness No. 1:	Signature	________________
	Print Name	________________
	Address	________________
	Date	________________
Witness No. 2:	Signature	________________
	Print Name	________________
	Address	________________
	Date	________________

Commentary: The *Substitute Decisions Act, 1992*, allows the client to appoint one or more attorneys to make decisions affecting his or her property. The authority may be general or may be restricted in some way. The client and the attorney(s) must be at least 18 years old.

There is no mandatory statutory form. The client may use any form as long as it complies with the statutory formalities.

Like the form for the continuing power of attorney for property set out in precedent L-1, the power of attorney made under the

Substitute Decisions Act, 1992, must be "enduring", that is, it must be expressed to be effective in the event of a subsequent incapacity.

Two witnesses are required. A witness must be at least 18 and cannot be the attorney, his or her spouse or partner, the spouse, partner or child of the client, a person the client treats as his or her child, or a person under guardianship.

L-4 POWER OF ATTORNEY FOR PERSONAL CARE.

Short description: A person is named to consent to treatment under the *Health Care Consent Act, 1996*, and to provide personal care under the *Substitute Decisions Act, 1992.*

POWER OF ATTORNEY FOR PERSONAL CARE

THIS POWER OF ATTORNEY FOR PERSONAL CARE is made by , of the City of , in the Municipality of .

APPOINTMENT

I. I APPOINT to be my attorney for personal care pursuant to the *Substitute Decisions Act, 1992*, S.O. 1992, c. 30.

AUTHORITY OF ATTORNEY

II. In accordance with the said Act, and in the full knowledge that my attorney for personal care will act in accordance with the wishes I have expressed, I authorize my attorney for personal care to make on my behalf any decisions concerning my personal care, and to give or refuse consent on my behalf to any treatment to which the *Health Care Consent Act, 1996*, S.O. 1996, c. 2, Sch. A, applies, as in 's discretion shall determine.

Substitution

III. If refuses to act, or is unable to act by reason of death, court removal, becoming incapacitated or resignation, or is not available to act at the time the necessity for a decision by an attorney for personal care arises concerning my personal care or treatment to which the *Health Care Consent Act, 1996*, applies (the question of necessity to be determined conclusively by a qualified medical person in attendance upon me), I SUBSTITUTE AND APPOINT to act as my attorney for personal care, in the place of and with all of the powers conferred upon the attorney appointed in paragraph I hereof.

Reimbursement for Expenses

IV. All expenses incurred by my attorney for personal care in carrying out his/her duties (including obtaining an assessment of my capacity, if required), shall be payable by me or my attorney for property out of my assets.

No Restrictions

V. This power of attorney for personal care is not subject to any conditions or restrictions and is given by me with the understanding that my attorney for personal care has a genuine concern for my welfare, and in full appreciation that he/she may be required to make decisions to which this power of attorney relates.

Other Powers of Attorney

VI. I retain the right to make subsequent multiple powers of attorney for personal care.

Revocation

VII. Any prior power of attorney for personal care or any prior power of attorney which affects my personal care given by me is revoked.

WITNESSES

VIII. We have signed this power of attorney in the presence of the person whose name appears above and in the presence of each other.

SIGNED BY:______________________________

on the day of , 19 , in the presence of the witnesses whose names appear below, and who signed on the same date.

______________________)
Witness)
)
______________________)
Print name and address)
)
______________________)
)
)
)
______________________)
Witness)
)
______________________)
Print name and address)
)
______________________)

Commentary: The *Substitute Decisions Act, 1992*, allows the client, who must be at least age 16, to appoint an attorney who will make personal care and consent to treatment decisions if the client becomes incapable of so doing.

The form of this precedent is not mandatory. The client is free to create his or her personalized document provided it is executed with the statutory formalities.

The attorney can be anyone 16 years or older, as long as he or she is not someone who provides health care or residential, social, training, advocacy or support services for compensation to your client, unless that person is a spouse or partner of the client. More than one attorney is permissible, and duties can be divided among them.

A witness to a power of attorney for personal care cannot be the attorney, his or her spouse or partner, the spouse, partner or child of the client, someone that the client treats as his or her child, a person under guardianship, or someone under 18.

L-5 DIRECTIVE FOR HEALTH CARE.

Short description: A person expresses his or her intentions regarding treatment and personal care decisions in the event that he or she becomes incapable of making those kinds of decisions.

POWER OF ATTORNEY FOR HEALTH CARE

I, , direct my family, my physician, my executor and all concerned others as follows:

1. If I am no longer able to make decisions for my own future, if I am no longer able to communicate, if I am unable to care for myself, if there is no reasonable expectation of my recovery from extreme physical or mental disability or incapacity, if circumstances exist that render me incapable of rational existence, if I am afflicted with [irreversible] injury, disease, illness or condition, then I want my attorneys to respect my wishes listed below.

Where the application of measures of artificial life support would primarily serve to prolong the moment of my death, then let this document stand as an expression of my thoughts, intentions, wishes and directions that I do not wish to endure any prolonged period of pain and suffering. I sign this document from my own free will while I am of sound mind and emotionally competent to make such decisions.

2. If any of these situations specified in paragraph 1 should arise, I direct that I be allowed to die and not

be kept alive by medications, artificial means or invasive measures of any kind.

3. Measures of extending life that I particularly do not wish, and which are to be withheld, withdrawn or discontinued include:

[(a) electrical or mechanical resuscitation of my heart;
(b) nutritional feedings;
(c) artificial mechanical respiration where my brain can no longer sustain breathing;
(d) radiation, chemotherapy and similar forms of treatment;
(e) treatment for an illness or disease which I contracted when I was already afflicted with a terminal illness.]

4. I do ask that medication be administered to alleviate pain, suffering or distress even though this may hasten the moment of my death.

5. I want the wishes and directions expressed in this power of attorney and the spirit of this document carried out to the fullest extent permitted by law. In so far as these are not legally enforceable, I nevertheless request that those responsible for me at such time will regard themselves as morally bound by these provisions, so that they will carry out these wishes to the fullest extent possible.

6. I would like to die at home rather than in an institution, if that does not impose an undue burden on those around me.

7. If any of the situations specified in this document should occur, I appoint as my attorney to carry out my thoughts and wishes, including obtaining a Court Order, if necessary, to discontinue or forbid artificial life support measures that would primarily serve to prolong the moment of my death.

8. If I should happen to be under the care of a physician whose moral, ethical or religious beliefs are not in sympathy with my wishes as expressed in this document, I direct my attorney to ask that physician to

withdraw from my care and to recommend another physician who agrees with my views.

9. No participant in the making or carrying out of this power of attorney, whether it be a health care provider, hospital administrator, friend, relative or any other person, shall be held responsible in any way, legally, professionally or morally, for any consequences arising from the implementation of my wishes.

In witness whereof I have signed my power of attorney this ______ day of ______, 19 .

______________________ ______________________
Signature of witness Signature of donor

____
Print name

____
Address

____
Occupation

____
Signature of witness

____
Print name

____
Address

____
Occupation

Commentary: An expression of intention can be useful for the attorney. It can be extremely difficult to make decisions without guidance. The wishes can be expressed orally or in writing, or be communicated in any other manner.

L-6 LIVING WILL.

Short description: The maker of this document expresses the wish that medical treatment be discontinued when there is no hope for recovery.

THE LIVING WILL OF ____________

It is the intent of this living Will to inform my family, my physician, my lawyer, my clergyman and anyone else who may become responsible for my health that I believe in the philosophy of death with dignity. Today we frequently hear the remark that North Americans enjoy the right to die with dignity. But all too often in actual medical practice these are shallow words.

The dying are still denied sufficient pain-killers. Thousands of others, either stricken with chronic disease or accident victims, are left immobilized. I do not want my family or physician to condone this type of existence for me. Life has no meaning under these conditions. There is a time to live and a time to die. To continue existing under such circumstances is senseless and needless psychological and physical agony.

I wish to stress the following points to those responsible for my medical care.

I know that this document is not legally binding, but I hope that my family and physicians will carry out the spirit of this agreement in view of my strong feelings on this matter.

I know that this document places a heavy responsibility on physicians. I suggest, therefore, that the decision to discontinue treatment be shared by three doctors.

I know that I may be under the care of a physician whose moral, ethical and/or religious doctrines demand that heroic measures be continued. I instruct my family in such an instance to request that physician's withdrawal from my care and to seek another physician who agrees that it is senseless to prolong life when there is no hope of recovery.

I know that the existing law does not allow doctors to practise active euthanasia. However, doctors are also not compelled to prolong life by heroic, extraordinary measures. Consequently, if there is no reasonable hope that medical treatment will assure my recovery from physical and mental disability, I want [heroic *or* all] measures discontinued.

I know that needless suffering occurs because of the ineffective use of pain-killers. In my final days, it is my desire to receive medication at regular intervals and in whatever dosage is needed to control pain. I wish this carried out even though it may hasten the moment of my death. Heroin may become a legal drug in Canada. If this happens, I wish to have this pain-killer administered during my final days.

I know that even stopping all care may not end my life in a reasonable time. With the exception of intravenous drips for pain-killers, I want all intravenous feedings stopped in the event that this should happen.

This living will is signed while I am fully cognizant of all the implications.

DATED this day of , 19 .

______________________ ______________________
Witness Signature of testator

____
Address

____
Witness

____
Address

Commentary: This document is useful as an expression of the intention of the maker and can be of great comfort to family and friends. The *Substitute Decisions Act, 1992*, says that the attorney for personal care must have regard to documents of this nature. In the drafting of a living will, the client should be invited to express his or her views in a personal way, unless this document is appropriate. It is not, however, a "form".

L-7 SPECIAL POWER OF ATTORNEY FOR THE PURCHASE OF PROPERTY.

Short description: This power given by the donor is limited to an event or a time period.

THIS SPECIAL POWER OF ATTORNEY is given on the day of , 19 , by of .

I APPOINT of [*or* of and of jointly *or* jointly and severally] to be my attorney(s) in accordance with the *Substitute Decisions Act, 1992*, S.O. 1992, c. 30 (the "Act"), and to do on my behalf anything that I can lawfully do by an attorney.

This power of attorney is subject to the following conditions and restrictions:

1. The power of attorney shall be exclusively for the purposes of negotiating and completing all matters necessary for the preparation and execution of all documents concerning the purchase of premises known municipally as , and , [Toronto], Ontario.
2. Without limiting the generality of the foregoing, the power shall extend to the entering into of an agreement of purchase and sale and the execution of all documentation necessary for the completion of any transaction contemplated therein.

3. Notwithstanding anything contained herein, this power of attorney shall permit the donee to release any and all possessory and/or proprietary rights I may have under the *Family Law Act*, R.S.O. 1990, c. F.3, relating to the property described in paragraph 1.
4. The power of attorney shall be for a period of days from the date on which this power of attorney is given. This special power of attorney is not intended to revoke the provisions of any general power of attorney made [of even date] given by in favour of , and the provisions of this special power of attorney are deemed to be amended so as not to revoke any of the provisions contained in the general power of attorney made [of even date].

If my spouse shall dispose of or encumber any interest in a matrimonial home in which I have a right to possession under Part II of the *Family Law Act*, I authorize the attorney(s) named in this power of attorney for me and in my name to consent to the transaction as provided for in subparagraph 21(1)(a) of the said Act.

In accordance with the Act, I declare that this power of attorney may be exercised during any subsequent legal incapacity on my part.

We have signed this power of attorney in the presence of the person whose name appears above and in the presence of each other.

SIGNED BY:________________ ________________

on the day of , 19 , in the presence of the witnesses whose names appear below, and who signed on the same date.

______________________)
Witness)
)
______________________)
Print name and address)
)
______________________)

	)
	)
	)
______________________________	)
Witness	)
	)
______________________________	)
Print name and address	)
	)
______________________________	)

Commentary: This is a useful power to be given to a named person when the donor is unable, for a limited purpose, to carry out a particular act such as the closing of a real estate transaction or managing a bank account while in Florida for the winter. To avoid any dispute over the extent of the exercise of the power, care must be taken to ensure that the drafting is crystal clear.

Chapter 7

EXECUTION, REPORTING, BILLING, REVIEW

The work is not over when the will has been drafted. The formalities of execution must be attended to. In Ontario an improperly executed will is no will at all. I like to supervise the execution. It gives me a chance to go over the will with the client and to ensure that he or she understands it and is signing voluntarily.

Following a discussion on execution, this chapter moves on to the follow-up steps to be taken after execution.

It is useful to review clients' wills from time to time, or at the very least to remind clients to undertake a review if there are significant changes in personal or financial affairs. As well, I try to do periodic mailers to will clients if there are important legislative changes. This takes organization and planning but is vastly assisted by computer programs to track and record clients and their wills.

M-1 LETTER SENDING OUT DRAFT DOCUMENTS FOR CLIENT'S CONSIDERATION.

Short description: You will send out to the client for his or her review all first drafts of the documents. It is important for the client to understand that the documents are not to be signed without further review and discussion.

, 19

Mr. and Mrs.
[*Address*]

Dear Mr. and Mrs. :

Re: Your Personal Planning

I am enclosing the following draft documents:

1. Draft Will of Mrs. .
2. Draft financial Power of Attorney of Mrs. in favour of Mr. .
3. Draft Power of Attorney for Personal Care of Mrs. in favour of Mr. .
4. Draft Will of Mr. .
5. Draft financial Power of Attorney of Mr. in favour of Mrs. .
6. Draft Power of Attorney for Personal Care of Mr. in favour of Mrs. .

Once you have had a chance to review these documents, please give me a call so that we can arrange to execute the originals. However, if I have misunderstood your instructions, or if you require changes, please let me know.

I look forward to hearing from you.

Yours very truly,

Commentary: Sending out the documents is intended only as a step in the chain of events leading up to execution of the formal will or power of attorney document. The solicitor must be able to prove that the client "knew and approved" the contents of the documents in order to establish the validity of the will.

M-2 INSTRUCTIONS FOR EXECUTION OF WILL.

Short description: This memorandum advises your client of the correct procedure for execution.

INSTRUCTIONS FOR THE EXECUTION OF YOUR WILL

In order that your Will be valid, it must be executed according to the strict requirements established by the *Succession Law Reform Act*, R.S.O. 1990, c. S.26. The following is the appropriate procedure.

- You and your witnesses must be present in the same room at the same time, and you must see one another execute the Will.
- The witnesses can be any persons over the age of eighteen years.
- *It is imperative that neither of the witnesses be a beneficiary or the spouse of a beneficiary named in the Will.*
- Insert the date in the first paragraph on page one of your Will, and place your initials in the right-hand margin on the same line.
- Place your initials in the right-hand margin at the bottom of all the pages of the Will.
- Sign the last page of the Will on the right-hand side, above where your name has been typed, using your normal signature.
- Each witness must then initial each page where you previously placed your initials, including the place where you inserted the date on page one.
- Each witness must then sign the last page of the Will on the left-hand side and include his or her

address and occupation. Ask the witnesses to sign as legibly as possible.

— Execute *only* the original Will (*no copies*).

Commentary: The requirements for correct execution of the will must be strictly complied with to ensure the validity of the will.

This precedent contemplates the client supervising the execution of the will. However, because I have seen clients with this memorandum (and indeed, non-probate lawyers) execute wills incorrectly in spite of the instructions, I have decided for my own practice that it would be negligent on my part, unless there were insurmountable impossibilities, not to supervise the execution of the wills which I draft for my clients. Accordingly, I put this precedent forward for the assistance of the supervisor and not for the assistance of the clients.

Part I of the *Succession Law Reform Act*, R.S.O. 1990, c. S.26, contains the formalities for execution and alteration of wills. Unlike some of the other common law jurisdictions in Canada, Ontario does not have provisions for "substantial compliance", and so a failure to follow the formalities of execution created by the legislation can invalidate a will.

Section 4 of the Act provides (with some exceptions) that a will is not valid unless: (a) it is signed at its end by the testator or by some other person in his or her presence and by his or her direction; (b) the testator makes or acknowledges the signature in the presence of two or more attesting witnesses present at the same time, and (c) two or more of the attesting witnesses subscribe the will in the presence of the testator. There are many cases which consider the requirement of "signing by the testator" and "signing at the end". While regard should be had to those cases, it is preferable to ensure that the formalities are met without exception.

Section 6 of the Act provides for the holograph will — a will made by the testator in his or her own handwriting and signature, without formality, and without the presence, attestation or signature of a witness.

Section 12 of the Act provides that if a beneficiary, the spouse of a beneficiary or the person claiming under either of them witnesses a will, the gift to the beneficiary, spouse or person claiming under is void, although the will itself is valid. There is a saving provision, however. If the court is satisfied that neither the witness nor the spouse of the witness exercised improper or undue influence upon the testator, the gift is not void. Obviously, though, it is easier to ensure that this event does not happen rather than to clean it up after the event.

M-3 INSTRUCTIONS FOR EXECUTION OF CODICIL.

Short description: As precedent M-2 does for a will, this precedent ensures that a codicil to a will is validly executed.

INSTRUCTIONS FOR THE EXECUTION OF YOUR CODICIL

In order that your Codicil be valid, it must be executed according to the strict requirements established by the *Succession Law Reform Act*, R.S.O. 1990, c. S.26. The following is the appropriate procedure.

— You and your witnesses must be present in the same room at the same time, and you must see one another execute the Codicil.

— The witnesses can be any persons over the age of eighteen years.

— *It is imperative that neither of the witnesses be a beneficiary or the spouse of a beneficiary named in the Will or Codicil.*

— Place your initials in the right-hand margin at the bottom of all the pages of the Codicil.

— Insert the date in the first paragraph on the last page of your Codicil, and place your initials in the right-hand margin on the same line.

- Sign the last page of the Codicil on the right-hand side, above where your name has been typed, using your normal signature.
- Each witness must then initial each page where you previously placed your initials, including the place where you inserted the date on the last page.
- Each witness must then sign the last page of the Codicil on the left-hand side and include his or her address and occupation. Ask the witnesses to sign as legibly as possible.
- Execute *only* the original Codicil (*no copies*).

Commentary: The commentary following precedent M-2 is equally applicable to this precedent.

M-4 AFFIDAVIT OF EXECUTION OF WILL.

Short description: This affidavit supports the execution of the will and makes the will exhibit "A" to the affidavit.

ONTARIO COURT (GENERAL DIVISION) AT

AFFIDAVIT OF EXECUTION OF A WILL

IN THE MATTER OF THE EXECUTION OF THE WILL OF

I, , of the [City] of , in the [Municipality/Regional Municipality/District] of

, and Province of Ontario, make oath and say:

1. On or about the day of , 19 , I was present and saw the paper writing annexed and marked as Exhibit "A" to this my Affidavit executed by .
2. At the time of execution, I knew such person, who was on that date of the full age of eighteen years to the best of my knowledge.
3. The said paper writing was executed by such person in the presence of , of the [City] of , in the [County] of , and Province of Ontario, and me, and we were both present at the same time, whereupon we did, in the presence of such person, attest and subscribe the said paper writing as witnesses.

SWORN before me at the)
[City] of , in the)
[Municipality] of ,)
and Province of Ontario,)
this day of)
, 19 .)

A Commissioner for Oaths, etc.	Signature of witness

Commentary: When a will or codicil is submitted to probate, it must be supported by an affidavit of one of the witnesses who will swear that he or she was present and saw the paper signed by the testator, that he or she knew the testator, that the testator was at least 18 years of age and that the other witness was present at the same time. The purpose of this affidavit is to satisfy the court that the formalities required by the *Succession Law Reform Act*, mentioned in precedent M-2, were met.

M-5 AFFIDAVIT OF EXECUTION OF CODICIL.

Short description: This affidavit supports the execution of a codicil and makes the codicil exhibit "A" to the affidavit.

ONTARIO COURT
(GENERAL DIVISION)
AT

AFFIDAVIT OF
EXECUTION OF A
CODICIL

IN THE MATTER OF THE EXECUTION OF THE CODICIL OF

I,   , of the [City] of   , in the [County] of   , and Province of Ontario, make oath and say:

1. On or about the   day of   , 19 , I was present and saw the paper writing annexed and marked as Exhibit "A" to this my Affidavit executed by   .
2. At the time of execution, I knew such person, who was on that date of the full age of eighteen years to the best of my knowledge.
3. The said paper writing was executed by such person in the presence of   , of the [City] of   , in the [County] of   , and Province of Ontario, and me, and we were both present at the same time, whereupon we did, in the presence of such person, attest and subscribe the said paper writing as witnesses.

SWORN before me at the)
[City] of , in the)
[Municipality] of ,)
and Province of Ontario,)
this day of)
, 19 .)

____________________ ____________________
A Commissioner for Oaths, etc. Signature of witness

Commentary: The commentary following precedent M-4 is equally applicable to this precedent.

M-6 REPORTING LETTER.

Short description: This letter acknowledges that original wills and powers of attorney have had their affidavits of execution completed and are in the vault. More importantly, it recommends to the client that he or she periodically review the will and keep the solicitor notified of changes in address, etc.

[*Name of client*]
[*Address*]

Dear :

Re:

I am pleased to advise that your original Will and Powers of Attorney have been placed in our vault for safe keeping, following the completion by us of affidavits of their execution. Since this completes all matters in connection with your estate planning, I am enclosing this statement of our account. I trust you will find it satisfactory.

If you have any questions or comments, please let me know.

A periodic review of your estate planning is essential. If changes should occur in your personal and financial affairs, you may need changes to your Will and other documents. As well, changes in federal and provincial legislation could affect your planning. I will try to keep you informed, but if you become aware, from the newspaper and other media, of new legislation which appears to affect you, please call me.

Finally, please keep me advised of changes in your address and/or telephone numbers.

Yours very truly,

Commentary: I usually keep my clients' wills and codicils in my vault for safe keeping. I recommend strongly against the client keeping these documents in a safe deposit box because it is only the executor who has the right of access to a deceased person's box. However, if his or her proof of appointment is in the box, then one must rely on the good offices of the bank manager to open the box. As well, if a client's will is in our vault, that will is safe from alteration or interference, not only by unhappy beneficiaries, but also by the testator during his or her lifetime. It is tempting to change the provisions of the will by writing on the original document, something which will not happen if the original is at the law firm.

You will see from the letter that I recommend periodic review. I also tell clients that, if there are changes in federal or provincial legislation, I will notify them, provided I can locate them. For example, when Ontario introduced its *Family Law Act, 1986*, S.O. 1986, c. 4, I wrote to all our clients suggesting that they review their wills and personal affairs under the circumstances created by the Act. This kind of notification can be a vast and expensive undertaking, but it is particularly useful to the clients. You need to be sure, though, if you tell clients you will contact them in the event of changing law, that you follow through on that commitment.

I mark on the copies of wills and other documents which are given to clients that those documents are copies only and that the originals are located in my vault. It is important that the copies clearly demonstrate the location of the original documents and the name of the lawyer who prepared them. I give the copies to my clients in an appropriate presentation envelope.

Section 2 of the *Estates Act*, R.S.O. 1990, c. E.21, provides that the local registrar of the Ontario Court (General Division) will act as a depository for wills and codicils. In Toronto, the local registrar is also the estate registrar for Ontario. Rule 74.02[1] of the *Rules of Civil Procedure*, R.R.O. 1990, Reg. 194, tells how a will is to be stored, the information that is to be given on the deposit envelope and the conditions for release of a will during the testator's life and after death. As a matter of interest, the archives contain wills going back over a hundred years.

M-7 ACCOUNT.

Short description: This precedent sets out a statement of account for the preparation of wills and powers of attorney.

GST Registration No.
File No.

[*Name of client*]
[*Address*]
[*Date*]

Dear :

THIS IS THE STATEMENT OF OUR ACCOUNT for professional services rendered to you in connection with your personal planning including:

— meeting with you to discuss your planning;

— preparation of draft Will for your consideration and review;

[1] Enacted O. Reg. 484/94, s. 12.

— preparation of draft Continuing Power of Attorney for Property for your consideration and review;

— [*specify any other documents and services*];

— attending with you for the purpose of reviewing and executing the original Will and original Continuing Power of Attorney for Property;

— preparation of the Affidavit of Execution of the Will and the Continuing Power of Attorney for Property and placing the original Will and Continuing Power of Attorney for Property in our vault for safe keeping;

— reporting to you.

OUR FEE:			$
FEE GST:		$	
DISBURSEMENTS:			
(a) [*Itemize disbursement*]	$		
(b) [*Itemize disbursement*]	$		$
DISBURSEMENT GST:		$	
TOTAL FEES AND DISBURSEMENTS:			$
TOTAL GST:			$
TOTAL AMOUNT DUE:			$

This is our account herein.

Commentary: I have included this precedent because I find that too often lawyers give away their estate planning work as a loss leader, with a consequence that this kind of planning is not always given sufficient attention. However, clients given a thorough and comprehensive approach to estate planning, such as that described in Chapter 1, will understand the scope of the process and may be billed accordingly.

An excellent audio tape to remind you to value your estates practice is from the February 1, 1989, trust and estate section meeting of the Canadian Bar Association. It is entitled "Marketing an Estate Practice". The meeting comprised several speakers who dwelt on the expectations of a client involved in the estate planning process. Among those speakers were the then dean of the University of Toronto Law School, Rob Prichard, Joe Dickstein of PPI Insurance and James Kennedy of Osler, Hoskin & Harcourt. The audio tape mentioned is available from the Canadian Bar Association (order number 5-88-603). I highly recommend it to you.

M-8 AFTER THE WILL IS SIGNED.

Short description: This information sheet is given to clients with the copies of their wills.

YOUR PERSONAL PLANNING

I. After your Will is signed

The following steps should be taken right away:

1. Let your executor and family members know where the original Will is.
2. Make and keep current a list of your assets and where they can be found.
3. List and keep current the names and addresses of your beneficiaries.
4. Keep your documents in one place, including the title to your home, personal agreements (such as divorce papers, separation agreements, marriage contracts, family trusts), and make sure that someone else knows where these documents can be found.

II. Reviewing your personal planning

Your Will and other planning should be reviewed on a regular basis. Your family circumstances may change, the laws may change or your mind may change about your beneficiaries.

I recommend that you review your planning at least once a year, every time that there are changes in your personal or financial affairs, or if you acquire property outside Canada.

If you want to change your Will, do not make any changes on the original Will. You can amend your Will by making a new Will. You can also amend it by a document called a Codicil. This document may be a formal document with two witnesses, or it may be wholly in your own handwriting (but make sure you understand the legal consequences of the changes you are making).

The law sometimes revokes your Will or parts of it when there are changes in your circumstances:

1. If you marry after the date of the Will, the Will is void at the option of your new spouse.
2. If you divorce, the gifts to your former spouse are void, and the Will is read as though your former spouse predeceased you, unless your Will expresses a different intention.
3. Making a new will revokes the previous Will.
4. Destroying your Will revokes it.

Commentary: Your work is not finished when the will is completed, stored for safe keeping and the account sent out. I give this information sheet to my clients to leave with their wills. The information assists them in organizing their documents and helps them to know when it is time for revisions or a new will.

INDEX